England

(1) THE MAN WITHIN 1929 *Sussex*
(2) IT'S A BATTLEFIELD 1934 *London*
(3) A GUN FOR SALE 1936 *London*
(4) BRIGHTON ROCK 1938 *Sussex*
(5) THE CONFIDENTIAL AGENT 1939 *London, Midlands and East Anglia*
(6) THE MINISTRY OF FEAR 1943 *London*
(7) THE END OF THE AFFAIR 1951 *London*
(8) TRAVELS WITH MY AUNT 1969 *Brighton*
(9) THE HUMAN FACTOR 1978 *London and Berkhamsted*

Continental Europe

(10) STAMBOUL TRAIN 1932 *Belgium and Germany*
(11) ENGLAND MADE ME 1935 *Sweden*
(12) THE THIRD MAN 1950 *Vienna*
(13) LOSER TAKES ALL 1955 *Monte Carlo*
(14) MAY WE BORROW YOUR HUSBAND? 1967 *Antibes*
(15) TRAVELS WITH MY AUNT 1969 *Boulogne and Paris*
(16) DR FISCHER OF GENEVA 1980 *Switzerland*
(17) MONSIGNOR QUIXOTE 1982 *Spain*
(18) THE TENTH MAN 1985 *Paris*

Africa

(19) THE HEART OF THE MATTER 1948 *Freetown, Sierra Leone*
(20) A BURNT-OUT CASE 1961 *Zaire*

Asia

(21) THE QUIET AMERICAN 1955 *Vietnam*

GRAHAM GREENE COUNTRY

GRAHAM GREENE COUNTRY

Visited by Paul Hogarth

Foreword and Commentary by Graham Greene

PAVILION
MICHAEL JOSEPH

First published in Great Britain
by Pavilion Books Limited
196 Shaftesbury Avenue,
London WC2H 8JL
in association with Michael Joseph Limited,
27 Wrights Lane, Kensington
London W8 5DZ

Designed by David Driver

Printed and bound in Italy by Arnoldo Mondadori

British Library Cataloguing
in Publication Data

Hogarth, Paul
Graham Greene country
1. Greene, Graham—Homes and haunts   2. Voyages
and travels
I. Title   II. Greene, Graham
910   PR6013.R44Z/
ISBN 1 85145 042 4

CONTENTS

My appreciative thanks are extended
to all those friends, colleagues and
personages who, in one way or another,
eased the progress of my work and
travels by their helpful advice and
hospitality, notably: Bridget Kitley,
London, for the synopses and research;
Nina Rudling, Stockholm *(England
Made Me)*; Dorothy Ritchie, Local
Studies Library, County Library,
Nottingham *(A Gun for Sale)*; Oscar and
Eileen Lowenstein, Brighton *(Brighton
Rock)*; Professor John Bailey,
Georgetown University, Washington
DC *(The Power and the Glory)*; Señor
Juan Moreira, Havana *(Our Man in
Havana)*; Professor Michel Lechat,
Université Catholique de Louvain,
Father Piet Hens and Sister Maria,
Léproserie de IYonda, Zaire, and M.
John-Paul Van Bellinghen, Belgian
Ambassador to the Court of St James *(A
Burnt-Out Case)*; Señor Juan Eduardo
Fleming, Chargé d'Affaires, Argentina
Section, Brazilian Embassy, London,
Robert Graham, Latin American editor,
Financial Times, and Señor Eduardo
Sefarian, Corrientes *(The Honorary
Consul)*; Maître Claude Soupert, Geneva
(Dr Fischer of Geneva); Father
Leopoldo Duran, Madrid, Toby Hogarth
and Señor Antonio Noquerias *(Monsig-
nor Quixote)* and Madame Meredith
Frappier, Paris *(The Tenth Man)*.
My thanks are also due to British
Airways for providing transport
facilities to Bangkok. Special thanks are
also due to Penguin Books for their
permission to reproduce the cover illustrations of their editions of the novels.
And last, but certainly not least, to
Mary Simmons and Eve Holroyd of
Twicker's World, who made light of the
sometimes bewildering number of
complex travel arrangements.
Graham Greene's novels are
presented in the chronological order in
which they were published. My travels
in 1985, however, took the most
convenient route at the best time of the
year for working outdoors. Hence my
diary entries are not in date order.

PAUL HOGARTH

To Graham Greene in admiration and affection
recalling our conversations on art, travel
and the pursuit of happiness

P H

FOREWORD

When I turn the pages of this album I feel a sense of awe at the daunting achievement of Paul Hogarth between his flights here and there across the world, and I feel too a sense of relief that I have not added still further to his travels by writing a novel after all my own journeys. At least he has not had to follow me to some trouble spots of which I did not write in fictional form – Kenya and the Mau Mau, Malaya in the Emergency, Israel in 1968, Nicaragua of the Sandinistas.

I find myself regarding his vivid evocative pictures with a certain sadness. It is not merely that so many scenes which I once described have changed in half a century, but that a novelist's memory is inevitably a bad one. No one forgets more easily than a novelist – it is his salvation to forget. An impression once snatched and put down on paper is no longer useful – it is despatched into the unconscious – even a character whom he has invented and lived with for more than a year may disappear completely into oblivion.

In his diary Hogarth follows me to Palmer's Pet Stores in Camden Town. I would have said before reading the diary that I had never heard of such a place, but apparently it appeared in one of my novels published over fifty years ago – a long time for a pet shop to survive in an area like Camden Town. Apparently a character of mine (I have to believe Paul Hogarth) called Bennett, a Communist leader, had a bed-sitting room above the pets, but I have no memory at all of someone called Bennett or of the part he played so long ago in a book of mine. And Miss Paterson whom Hogarth tracks down to a cemetery in Boulogne, who is she? These are not the only ones who owe their life now, not to the author but to the artist who has followed me like a detective after a criminal. And a writer is after all a kind of criminal without a conscience. How many people have died at his hands and been forgotten by the killer?

It is a relief when one of his pictures, entailing no long journey to Hanoi or Corrientes, coincides exactly with my memory and Harston House in Cambridgeshire releases from my sub-conscious a host of happy memories of childhood summers, of hide-and-seek in the Dark Walk and the rainy sound of the fountain, of the silver birches and the island in the pond, so different from the violent world of *The Ministry of Fear* in which it momentarily appears.

GRAHAM GREENE

A WORD FROM THE ARTIST

My travels during the fifties and sixties were demanding enough. I recall riding some thirty miles on a mountain pony to draw a Buddhist monastery in China's Great West; driving and drawing across the length and breadth of Ireland with Brendan Behan; covering rodeos in Canada's Wild West for *Sports Illustrated;* drawing bankers and tycoons for *Fortune* from Brussels to Barcelona, and much else.

Such experiences, I have discovered, pale beside those encountered while travelling in Graham Greene Country, as you will discover when reading my diary. Now I was involved with a year-long odyssey of 50,000 miles, encompassing four continents, over twenty countries and some fifty towns and cities.

On every leg of my travels, whenever I boarded a jet plane that whisked me over an ocean or jungle in hours instead of days, I'd think of the long, arduous, seminal journeys that Greene himself had made over forty years ago by ship and train. His background as a journalist, especially as a foreign correspondent, had led him to use the places he knew well, had lived in, or simply visited, as settings or locations for his novels. Neighbourhoods, towns and cities, are usually carefully described:

sometimes correctly, sometimes fictitiously. It was fascinating to discover that so much still existed.

Following in his footsteps involved me in tackling every kind of subject under the most diverse conditions and circumstances. It also revived my own sense of moral outrage. The *barrios* of Latin America, for example, brought back memories of South Africa in 1956, when I depicted life in the shanty towns of Capetown, Port Elizabeth and Johannesburg. It isn't easy to make such drawings. But confronted with the challenge of interpreting Greene's Third World novels I made the most of the occasional opportunity to do so.

Looking back on my travels, I realize that what initially attracted me towards Graham Greene's writing was his acute awareness of social contexts; used almost like theatrical backdrops for his narratives. It was a quality that appealed to my own conscience as well as my pencil. It was the same quality that had inspired my jacket illustrations for the Penguin editions of his novels. Without (I hope) sounding too patronizing, this book is ideal for anyone looking for a way to understand what brings a writer and an artist together.

PAUL HOGARTH

[THE MAN WITHIN]

Andrews, a coward, angered by the taunts of his fellow smugglers, betrays them to the customs officers. In the resulting fight an officer is killed and now many of the men await trial for murder but Carlyon, Andrews' erstwhile mentor, has escaped and seeks revenge. Andrews is sheltered by Elizabeth, a wise and beautiful young recluse, who persuades him to testify against the men, for she believes this act of courage will make a man out of the weak and self-pitying boy who had become a smuggler in order to appease his bullying father.

Andrews makes his way to the Assizes at Lewes where, much to popular distaste, he testifies against his former companions. But the smugglers convince the jury that only one of them is guilty of the murder; that he – a half-witted boy – had a long standing vendetta with the murdered gauger.

Aware of their common danger, Andrews makes his way back to Elizabeth and they declare their love for one another. But the smugglers seek them out and Andrews flees. Elizabeth, terrified of the men and desolated by Andrews' defection, kills herself. When Andrews, his courage returning, creeps back he finds Carlyon meditating over Elizabeth's body and for a moment the men are united by grief and their mutual respect for the girl. After Carlyon disappears, Andrews redeems himself by confessing to the police that he is guilty of Elizabeth's murder and he knows that, although the gallows are in sight, he has become a man at last.

"The down all around him was empty and refreshingly safe, and though danger might be lurking in the world below, it was dwarfed by distance. Somewhere twelve miles away lay Lewes, but for a little he need have no care of that. He was perched high up upon a safe instant of time and he clung hard to that instant, drowning all thought in mere sensation, the sight of the country unrolled like a coloured map below him, the feel of warmth creeping from neck to spine. In that long wash of sun, which left the moon an indistinct wraith in the transparent, fragile blue, lay a first hint of spring, and in the breeze, salt from the Channel, hidden from sight by yet another ridge of down, gorse-laden, prophesying green."

Graham Greene writes:
'My first published book I would gladly forget and yet the first too poetic sentence obstinately remains in my fading memory to shame me. "He came over the top of the down as the last light failed and could almost have cried with relief at sight of the wood below." '

Storm over Ditchling Beacon, Sussex

DIARY

Monday, August 19

Drive down to Sussex, the setting of Greene's first published novel, *The Man Within*. My first stop is Ditchling Beacon, and, weather and time permitting, to walk along the Downs to Harry's Mount. The Beacon doesn't impress me at first. It looks too soft and peaceful. Sudden change in the weather stops me from attempting the walk but transforms the look of the landscape. Rain clouds gather and the Beacon becomes a dramatic setting for Andrews' decision to reach Lewes that night and testify against his fellow smugglers.

I reach Lewes myself by car in the afternoon, and, just before sunset, get most of its magnificent castle drawn from two positions. The first from Westgate, the street below. The second from Pipe Passage, a path around the castle which enables me to see the massive, flint-studded walls in more detail, as the evening light fades.

Tuesday, August 20

The smugglers are tried at the Assize Court, now the County Hall, opposite the historic White Hart Inn (now Hotel) on the High Street. The square classical courthouse was built between 1808-12 and became the scene of many trials of smugglers a century and a half ago. The White Hart, also described in the novel, is a fine coaching inn with a Georgian façade, which dates from Elizabethan times.

Andrews, on his way to the High Street (where he falls into the clutches of Farne, agent of Sir Henry Merriman, prosecuting counsel determined to hang the smugglers), walks down Pipe Passage from the castle. This comes out opposite Keere Street ('Keerie Street'), a narrow plunging lane with an unexpected view of the English Channel on the far horizon. Unable to resist drawing the leaning ship-like houses and view beyond, I make it the last of my four scenes.

"*A little after midnight it began to rain, a dull steady dripping rain which never ceased. The sun rose, but not into sight. Grey banked clouds slowly appeared, and that was the one sign of day. Along Lewes High Street there was no sound save the regular drip, drip of water from pipes and gables and sign boards. Water streamed from the hair, the robes and the sword of the fat stone Justice on the Assize Court, as though she had just risen from the leaden waves of a 'pleasure resort', like Venus out of the Mediterranean. Unperturbed by cold and damp she stared across the street at the windows of the White Hart with an expressionless gaze. A blind was raised and a young man looked out for a moment at the street. Through another window the fading light of a candle could be seen moving upwards, as an elderly, sharp-featured man mounted the stairs to bed. The flames of the two street lamps ceased to be bright gold breaches in the dark and became finally a faint yellow smear on a grey page. Presently an elderly man shuffled along the pavement and turned them out. By order of Lewes Corporation day had officially begun.*

For several hours yet there was no movement of human beings in the street. A thin grey cat trod delicately along the gutter in a kind of dignified despondency, and a dog came trotting from a side turning, tail erect in spite of the rain. The cat leapt up three steps of a house and stood with bristling curved back, spitting defiance, while the dog, crouching close to the ground, barked in short, sharp bursts, more for amusement than for any real enmity. The blind of the White Hart was again raised and the same young man looked out, watching the by-play with an intent interest."

County Hall, Lewes, Sussex

Keere Street, Lewes, Sussex

"*There were few persons about in the street, which was like the deck of a sleeping ship lit by two lamps, fore and aft, and on each side a sudden fall into a dark sea. Opposite him two old houses leant crazily towards each other, almost touching above the narrow lane called Keerie Street, which dived chaotically into the night – a few confused squares and oblongs of inn signs, six steep feet of cobbles and then vacancy. Out beyond, but he could not see, was Newhaven and the Channel, France.*"

Graham Greene writes:
'How extraordinary that after nearly sixty years rickety Keere Street still survives.'

Lewes Castle, Sussex

"He looked every now and then at the castle which dominated Lewes from its hill. When it should be cloaked from sight he would go down. It seemed an endless while and it was very cold. The prospect of returning that night the way he had come, his promise fulfilled, grew uninviting. Besides, what welcome would he get from Elizabeth after so literal a fulfilment? There could be no great danger, he persuaded himself, in staying one night in Lewes. He knew from experience that there were many inns, and fortune could hardly deal so ill with him as to bring him face to face with anyone he knew. Carlyon would not dare to enter Lewes when the Assizes were so imminent and the town full of officers.

The shadows had fallen over the town and he could no longer see the castle, save as an indistinct hump or a shrugged shoulder. He began to walk down by a path longer than it had seemed in the silver light. By the time he had reached the first straggling houses, darkness was complete, pierced here and there by the yellow flicker of oil lamps, crowned by dingy pinnacles of smoke from the lengthening wicks. Cautiously he made his way into the High Street, and stood for a while in the shadow of a doorway, probing his mind for the position of the various inns."

[STAMBOUL TRAIN]

Coral, a chorus girl, Myatt, a young Jewish business-man, Czinner, a revolutionary, and Janet, who is trying to escape from an unsatisfactory relationship with a lesbian journalist, Miss Warren, travel together on the Orient Express one winter in the early 1930's. Coral believes she has found warmth and care from Myatt who is genuinely touched by her. Czinner is pursued relentlessly by Miss Warren, who has recognized him as a former leader of the Yugoslavian social democratic party who went to ground five years earlier after having been a key witness in a political trial.

Miss Warren, discovering that Czinner is returning to Belgrade in order to mastermind a revolution, hopes to win herself a front page story which will command the respect and love of Janet. The uprising in Belgrade is premature and unsuccessful and unnoticed by the travellers. Czinner is arrested and Coral becomes accidentally involved in Czinner's attempt to escape. She then witnesses his subsequent death and her frail heart, which had longed for Myatt's warmth and strength, gives up the unequal struggle.

Myatt, who had been concerned about Coral's disappearance, tries to find her but is himself found by Janet who will be, after all, a fiancée of better status than a naive chorus girl. Much of what had seemed trivial or comic at the outset of the journey has become tragic at its conclusion.

Purser on the Dover-Ostend Ferry

"The purser took the last landing-card in his hand and watched the passengers cross the grey wet quay, over a wilderness of rails and points, round the corners of abandoned trucks. They went with coat-collars turned up and hunched shoulders; on the tables in the long coaches lamps were lit and glowed through the rain like a chain of blue beads. A giant crane swept and descended, and the clatter of the winch drowned for a moment the pervading sounds of water, water falling from the overcast sky, water washing against the sides of channel steamer and quay. It was half past four in the afternoon."

Graham Greene writes:
'One passenger who joined the train caused me a lot of trouble. I described him as a popular novelist who compared himself with Dickens, and J B Priestley identified himself with the character. He threatened my publisher with a libel action and I was forced to change the name Dickens to Chaucer.'

Boat Train leaving Ostend Station

Waiter and waitress on the Dover-Ostend Ferry

DIARY

Monday, October 21

Even when I first read *Stamboul Train* many years ago, I'd visualized the grandiose railway stations which marked the stately progress of the Orient Express through Europe to Istanbul. I'd interpret the novel with a series of magnificent watercolours of those stations. But Greene objected. I shouldn't go any further east than Cologne he said. 'Why?' I said blankly. The advance, he replied, hadn't permitted going any further on a third-class ticket. The rest, he went on, was written with the help of Karl Baedeker.

So here I am, on a glorious October morning, standing in a long queue at Victoria Station with what seems to be an army of noisy German teenagers, returning from summer holidays. The time is 09.30, destination Cologne via the Dover-Ostend ferry. I am travelling first-class in the naive hope that this will enable me to avoid the madding crowd and talk to possible counterparts of Dr Czinner, Carleton Myatt, Coral Musker, Janet Pardoe and Mabel Warren. But there is no-one. I bury my nose in *Stamboul Train* and the time passes. I look up and suddenly there's a breathtaking view of the white cliffs of Dover.

After a smooth crossing, land at Ostend, but I don't as yet feel any Greenesian vibrations. Nothing could be more mundane, although I have made several sketches of pursers, waitresses and the like during the crossing. Decide to break the ice and get to work on an impression of a modern express, an electric train gliding along under a spider's web of black power cables. The old Orient Express must have looked much more dramatic, as it was hauled by huge steam-powered locomotives.

Continue to Bruges. Although the beauty of its skyline is glimpsed from the railway, I feel the reader should be given a closer look. Break journey and stay night in a cosy warren-like *pension* in Wollestraat. Feel like a traitor to train-travel as I sit down to an incredibly delicious dinner.

Hotel Excelsior Bar, Cologne

" 'But of course, dear, I don't mind your being drunk,' said Janet Pardoe. The clock above Cologne station struck one, and a waiter began to turn out the lights on the terrace of the Excelsior. 'Look, dear, let me put your tie straight.' She leant across the table and adjusted Mabel Warren's tie.

'We've lived together for three years,' Miss Warren began to say in a deep melancholy voice, 'and I have never yet spoken to you harshly.'

Janet Pardoe put a little scent behind her ears. 'For heaven's sake, darling, look at the time. The train leaves in half an hour, and I've got to get my bags, and you've got to get your interview. Do drink up your gin and come along.' "

Guard at Ostend

Guard at Bruges

"Presently the engine settled smoothly to its work, the driver brought the cut-off back, and the last of the sun came out as the train passed through Bruges, the regulator closed, coasting with little steam. The sunset lit up tall dripping walls, alleys with stagnant water radiant for a moment with liquid light. Somewhere within the dingy casing lay the ancient city, like a notorious jewel, too stared at, talked of, trafficked over."

Quay of the Rosary, Bruges

DIARY

Tuesday, October 22

Another crisp autumn day. Spend it drawing Bruges. The old city of Hans Memling and Jan van Eyck is a miracle of survival. Largely Medieval but with the occasional Baroque palace. Depict massed cluster of ancient houses dominated by the giant Belfry Tower from the Rozenhoedkaai (Quay of the Rosary). Crocodiles of school-children march backwards and forwards, chattering in English, French and German. Japanese business-men, no doubt thinking I too was a survival, take photographs of me at work. Thurber-like American couples stand and argue affectionately with one another.

Wednesday, October 23

Continue train journey to Cologne. Few fellow-passengers. Occasionally a business-man comes and goes. But no-one really interesting. Am left to contemplate passing landscape which changes from fertile farmland to cosy suburbia. Look in vain for the 'great blastfurnaces of Liège' that Greene so tellingly describes as looking 'like ancient castles burning in a border raid'. German business-man informs me that they have long since been demolished. But then, some enormous overgrown slag-heaps come into view on the western fringes of Liège. The blastfurnaces have become Bronze Age barrows.

Thursday, October 24

Stamboul Train is the most difficult of all Greene's novels to interpret, because it was set in the early thirties in locations that don't exist anymore. Europe's grand old mainline railway stations are no longer halls of mystery and intrigue. Czinner, Myatt, Musker, Pardoe and Warren all would travel by air today. But this is not to say I didn't find a few haunting reminders. Ironically, I discovered these in Cologne in a rebuilt *Zentralbahnhof*, a station building of great style, and the nearby Excelsior Hotel. Here, in the Excelsior's ornate bar, a setting which Greene used for Janet Pardoe and Mabel Warren, one can still imagine the two getting high on cocktails.

Street toy vendor, Cologne

"All the way down the Rhine was her [Mabel Warren's] province; there wasn't a town of any size between Cologne and Mainz where she hadn't sought out human interest, forcing dramatic phrases on to the lips of sullen men, pathos into mouths of women too overcome with grief to speak at all."

Cologne Cathedral and Bahnhof

27

During a fracas at a pre-war political meeting Drover, a Communist bus driver, believing a policeman was about to hit his wife, stabbed him to death. Now Drover has lost his appeal against his death sentence, his wife despairs, and his brother Conrad, overwhelmed by the responsibility cast upon him and his wife's sister, seeks re-affirmation of life through sex.

"The truth is nobody cares about anything but his own troubles. Everybody is too busy fighting his own battle to think of the next man..." The family believe the Communist party will help them but the Party does not feel there is enough political capital to be gained from it. They try to interest the press but the story has died. They try to find an influential figure who will sway the frigid mind of the Assistant Commissioner who has been given overall responsibility for the case by the Home Office, but he is resistant.

Conrad, jealous of the quiet stoicism of his brother, maddened by his own inadequacy and his betraying, desperate and mistaken coupling with his brother's lonely wife, tries to reassert his manhood by shooting the Assistant Commissioner, but his gun is defective and he is run down by a passing car. Conrad dies before he hears the news that his brother's sentence has been commuted to eighteen years' imprisonment. Drover's wife will be middle-aged when he is released and he, who had made an ineffective attempt at suicide when he heard of his life sentence, will be a broken man.

"The clock in the high tower struck six-thirty, and the siren cried through the dusk. No one responded; overtime was being worked in the match factory off Battersea Rise, but the siren, which was connected electrically with the clock, screamed on for a minute and a half while a hundred blue-and-white matchboxes jumped from the machines on to a great moving stair which drew them with slow solemnity, as if they were small coffins in a crematorium, to the blast of heat in the drying chamber. The hundred and fifty girls in the machine-room worked with the regularity of a blood beat; a hand to the left, a hand to the right, the pressure of a foot; a damp box flew out, turned in the air, and fell on the moving stair. It was impossible to hear the boxes falling, or a voice speaking, because of the noise of the machines, the machines in the hall, the machines in the cellar where tree trunks uncurled into thin strips of wood, the machines in the room above, where on a revolving band the pink-headed matches marched fifty deep up towards the ceiling, down towards the sulphur vats."

Graham Greene writes:
'The Gloucester factory came my way because while I was living in Gloucestershire in 1932 a box of matches exploded in my hand. I wrote a letter of complaint and promptly received enough matches to last me for a year and an invitation to visit the factory. I had already visited Wandsworth Prison and my visit to the factory in Gloucester provided me with an ironic contrast for the novel I was writing. How much a novelist owes to lucky breaks.'

Old Bryant & May factory, Gloucester

DIARY

Wednesday, July 10

Wandsworth Prison, a location described in *It's a Battlefield*, is one of those grim Victorian citadels of correction. Drover, the Communist bus driver, is held here pending trial for murder. But how to draw it? A giant concrete wall conceals the entrance gate. Guards with large dogs patrol the perimeter segment by segment. I'm almost on the point of abandoning the idea when I see a possible loophole in these security precautions.

Greatly daring, I walk up a private road to the rear of the prison. Glimpse stalwart guard with large dog in distance. Beat hasty retreat and expect to be followed. But no, I'm not followed or even noticed. Retrace my steps and discover verdant enclave from which to draw. Take out folding stool from portfolio and get to work. Drawing goes well for thirty minutes or so. Then notice pair of large-size black boots in front of sketchbook. Find myself eyeball to eyeball with gimlet-eyed guard restraining panting Alsation. Following dialogue takes place:

'Is it alright to make a sketch, officer? – it's for a book with Graham Greene.'

'Niver 'eard of 'im,' the guard barks, 'got any ID?'

Produce my Royal Academy of Arts identity card which is duly examined.

'Alright,' the guard says, 'but be quick abart it.'

Wednesday, July 17

Walk from my studio in Primrose Hill to draw Palmer's Pet Store in Parkway, Camden Town. As if proud of its niche in Greene country, the street looks its seedy best. The shop is described in the novel as 'a zoological shop', and still exists after all this time. On the floor above are the lodgings, the bed-sitter of the Communist leader, Bennett.

" 'Mr Bennett?' he said to the man on the ground floor. 'I want to see him. Is he in?' Dogs barked and bit each other in a zoological shop across the way, and very faintly, because the traffic was almost stilled, it was possible to hear the lions in Regent's Park roaring to be fed."

Palmer's Pet Store, Camden Town

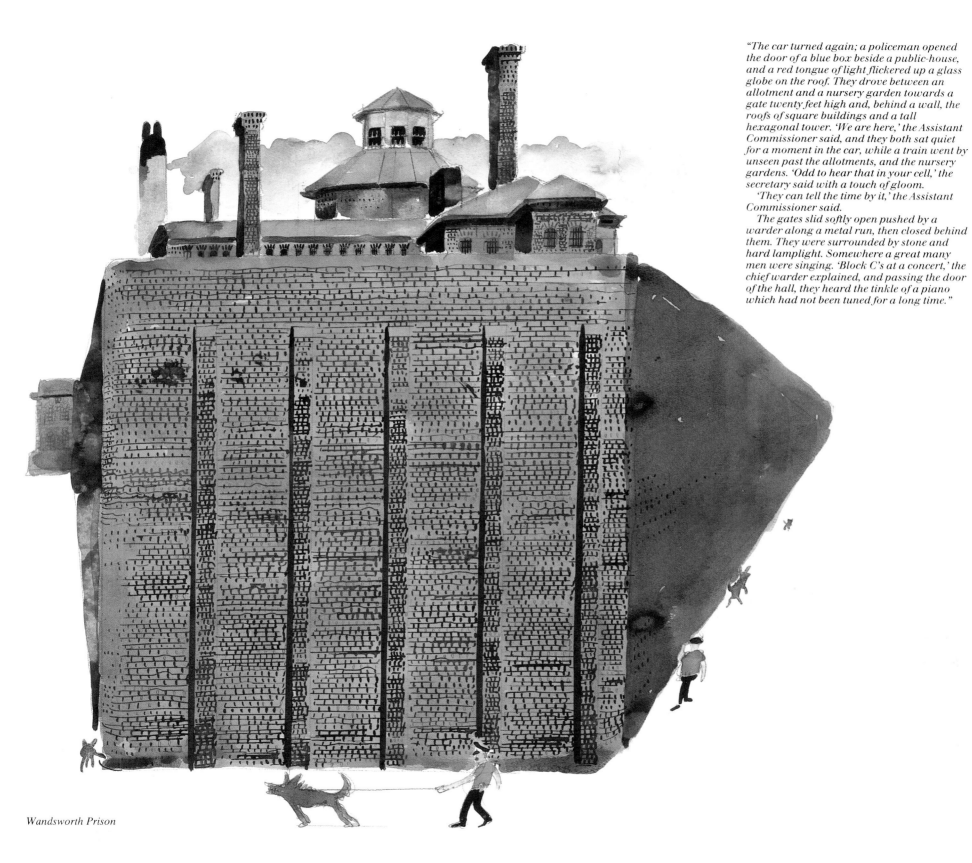

"The car turned again; a policeman opened the door of a blue box beside a public-house, and a red tongue of light flickered up a glass globe on the roof. They drove between an allotment and a nursery garden towards a gate twenty feet high and, behind a wall, the roofs of square buildings and a tall hexagonal tower. 'We are here,' the Assistant Commissioner said, and they both sat quiet for a moment in the car, while a train went by unseen past the allotments, and the nursery gardens. 'Odd to hear that in your cell,' the secretary said with a touch of gloom.

'They can tell the time by it,' the Assistant Commissioner said.

The gates slid softly open pushed by a warder along a metal run, then closed behind them. They were surrounded by stone and hard lamplight. Somewhere a great many men were singing. 'Block C's at a concert,' the chief warder explained, and passing the door of the hall, they heard the tinkle of a piano which had not been tuned for a long time."

Wandsworth Prison

DIARY

Tuesday, August 6

Make thumbnail sketches of prostitutes in Old Compton Street neighbourhood. Soho prostitutes appear in many of Greene's early novels with London settings; especially *It's a Battlefield*. In the thirties, many Soho ladies of the night were Belgian or French, or pretended to be. Nowadays most are prosaically Brit from the provinces. Younger ones dress in combinations of sadio-masochist gear and punk hair-do's, giving them the look of expelled denizens from the lower reaches of Faerie.

Thursday, August 15

Spend afternoon in Fitzrovia. Depict frontage of Fitzroy Tavern, Charlotte Street. The once celebrated pub was the meeting-place of the local working-class and the *literati* of the thirties. In his novel, Greene has the journalist Conder invite Kay Rimmer and Jules Briton to join him for a drink here in order to find out more about the unfortunate Drover. I recall the Fitzroy in the late forties: listening to the cut-and-thrust talk of a white-haired and bulbous-nosed Augustus John with John Davenport, Randall Swingler and a noisy Dylan Thomas in attendance.

Saturday, August 24

A fresh and gusty morning in Trafalgar Square which evokes another memory of London: the flying weekend visits with my parents as a boy. Arguments and aching feet. I've drawn the Square before but not for some years. It has changed very little. Still the Mecca of visitors: parents with children, clusters of shrieking teenagers, Australian retirees and Commonwealth immigrants. All enjoying the sights of the Square as though at a carnival.

Saturday, September 28

I'm spending the weekend in the Cotswolds. Since midday I've been walking around Chipping Campden, a picturesque large village of Medieval stone houses and thatched cottages nestling in the hills. In one such cottage on the edge of the village 'down a muddy lane' which Greene rented for a pound a week, the author worked on *It's a Battlefield*. There was no electric light, only oil lamps which were not always easy to ignite and which smoked if left to their idiosyncratic devices. One night, a defective box of matches nearly caused a disaster. Greene wrote a letter of protest to the manager of Bryant & May's 'England's Glory' match factory in nearby Gloucester. An incident which not only resulted in an invitation to visit the factory plus a free gross of perfect matches, but provided Greene with the material he needed in order to describe the arduous life of the match girls which he placed in Battersea.

Sunday, September 29

On to Gloucester to find the factory. The surrounding countryside is exquisitely autumnal: misty valleys, ancient stone walls, ancestral homes and more picturesque villages. Regrettably, they don't form part of Graham Greene Country and I press on to Bristol Road where lo and behold, I find that the match factory still exists. Although no longer producing matches, its 'England's Glory' logo is still in place.

"The street was full of people, laughing and going home. Jules longed to be with them. He said to Conder: 'There's Kay,' and to Kay: 'This is Conder.' Conder took off his hat and Kay's eyes rested with distress, boredom, a veiled malevolence on the bald head.

'Can we see you home?' Conder asked.

'But I don't want to go home yet,' Kay said. 'It's early.' She leant against the lamp-post and pressed her cheek against the iron.

'Come to the park then,' Jules said.

'It'll be cold.'

'A café.'

'Both of you come with me,' Conder said, 'and have a drink at the "Fitzroy".'

'I've had too many drinks at the "Fitzroy". Can't you suggest something new, something exciting?'"

The Fitzroy Tavern, Charlotte Street

Soho prostitute

"They packed into a single car. The great lit globe of the Coliseum balanced above the restaurants and the cafés and the public-houses in St Martin's Lane. Round and round Trafalgar Square the buses went like circus horses. The high squeal of the Wolseley's hooter pierced through a traffic block; cars ground their brakes, a policeman raised his hand, and they were shaken out into Charing Cross Road temporarily bare of traffic. The whores flowed down one pavement and up another; flat dago faces printed on song sheets filled the window of a music shop and a salesman inside played with passionate melancholy: 'My Baby Don't Care'. A row of men peered into peepshows, and 'A Night in Paris' and 'What the Butler Saw' and 'For Women Only' rattled and whined and jolted and stuck."

Trafalgar Square

[ENGLAND MADE ME]

Kate will do anything to help her charming confidence trickster twin brother Anthony and to have him near her. She makes herself invaluable to Krogh, a powerful, isolated Swedish financier, acting as his secretary, hostess and lover and then persuades him to take on Anthony as a bodyguard. Anthony, pleased to have a period of security, is happy to stay in Stockholm for a while. Without wasting any time he starts an affair with ungainly, vulnerable Loo and secures Minty, a seedy, unscrupulous, misogynistic journalist, as a drinking partner.

Anthony can accept minor acts of opportunism and immorality but he is shocked when he discovers that Krogh will stop at nothing to further his empire. He is appalled that Kate can accept it and he cannot believe that she will even accept marriage to Krogh for his sake, such is her intense and exclusive love for her twin. To offset this shadow of incest he becomes very involved with Loo and when she returns to England he decides to follow her, but not before he has betrayed Krogh to Minty who wins a scoop at Krogh's expense. Anthony pays for this with his life and Kate, desolated by his death, has no longer any reason to stay with Krogh. She leaves Sweden for Europe – 'simply moving on. Like Anthony'.

"Across the sky stretched the hillside lights of Djurgården, the restaurants, the high tower in Skansen, the turrets and the switchbacks in Tivoli. A thin blue mist crawled from the water, covering the motor-boats, creeping half-way to the riding lights of the steamers. An English cruising liner lay opposite the Grand Hotel, its white paint glowing in the light of the street lamps, and through the cordage Krogh could see the tables laid, the waiters carrying flowers, the line of taxis on the North Strand. On the terrace of the palace a sentry passed and repassed, his bayonet caught the lamplight, the mist came up over the terrace to his feet. The damp air held the music from every quarter suspended, a skeleton of music above an autumnal decay."

Graham Greene writes:
'I had been unlucky in my contacts during my first stay in Stockholm in 1934 for the purposes of this book. Later in the fifties I found myself very happy there and became for a while almost a commuter. Then I regretted my earlier rather ignorant impression.'

Djurgården with Nordiska Museet from Strandvägen

35

Gustavus Adolphus Statue

Tuesday, June 18

Arrive at Stockholm, the setting of *England Made Me,* Greene's fifth published novel. After the turmoil of Central and South America previously visited, Sweden is like landing on another planet. Here, everything functions with a minimum of fuss and effort, and always on time. The airport bus glides through dense pine forests towards a city which appears to be a fascinating mixture of Hanseatic and Venetian. I'm a guest in a friend's flat close to the huge old park called Djurgården and much of Graham Greene's Stockholm.

Wednesday, June 19

The city has such great beauty. Profusion of lakes make evocative settings for numerous Baroque towers, delicate spires and Gothic gables. Hundreds of sailing ships and motorboats float at their moorings along picturesque quays: thickets of masts are silhouetted against a pale cobalt summer sky. For once, find it difficult to visualize Stockholm as the background for a Greenesian plot: the machinations of the megalomaniac tycoon Krogh, and the problems of Anthony and his adoring sister, Kate. How could such a delightful city be anything other than a cradle for the good life?

"He could see the lights in the square balconied block where he had his flat on the Norr Mälarstrand. The breadth of Lake Mälaren divided him from the workmen's quarters on the other bank. From his drawing-room window he could watch the canal liners arriving from Gothenburg with their load of foreign passengers. They had passed the place where he was born, they emerged at dusk unobtrusively from the heart of Sweden, from the silver birch woods round Lake Vätten, the coloured wooden cottages, the small landing stages where the chickens pecked for worms in soil spread thinly over rock. Krogh, the internationalist, who had worked in factories all over America and France, who could speak English and German as well as he could speak Swedish, who had lent money to every European Government, watched them of an evening sidle in to moor opposite the City Hall with a sense of something lost, neglected, stubbornly alive."

Drottingham boat pier

Norr Mälarstrand, Stockholm

Old phone box, Djurgården

DIARY

Thursday, June 20

Walk along Strandvägen to the Opera House. Attracted by the stylish equestrian statue of Gustavus Adolphus, 'the grey monarch', which faces the North Bridge and Russia. Punks pass under the huge statue like white-faded pixies. Swedish punks are strangely inoffensive. They appear to be similar to our London punks, but are mainly middle-class so behave more like hippies. They spend their time sitting around in parks chatting or staring into space, high on marijuana.

On to Norr Mälarstrand. I look for an apartment house in which Krogh might have lived: overlooking Lake Mälaren where 'from his drawing-room window he could watch the canal liners arriving from Gothenburg with their load of foreign passengers'. Faced with a large selection: mostly in an intimidating and massive style which might be dubbed North European baronial. Choose a square-looking specimen with a mansard-cum-conical tower and ornate cast-iron balconies.

Saturday, June 22

Spend the day in Djurgården, which contains, amongst many other things, Skansen, an anthropological complex, and Tivoli, an amusement park. Among the grey rocks and silver trees of Skansen, I hear in Greene's words 'the gentle creaking of the wooden boards' under the feet of country people, performing folk-dances to old Swedish airs. Reminiscent of a John Ford Western. I depict the Hazelius Gate, its main entrance. Skansen attracts not only the elderly recalling their roots but lovers and families. It's the traditional place to visit during *Midsommarfest*.

Tivoli, on the other hand, is a great deal less educational. Although more up-to-date and less downmarket than Palace Pier, Brighton, it nonetheless presents the same deceptive spectacle. People of all ages mill aimlessly about. Pimply youths fall prey to the attractions of shooting arcades.

" 'I'll come with you,' Anthony said, 'I've got to talk to you. We'll find somewhere to sit. Skansen. Is it far to Skansen?' "

Tivoli gardens

Skansen, The Hazelius Gate

[A GUN *for* SALE]

During the thirties Sir Marcus, the corrupt owner of an armaments company, working through middle man Cholmondeley, hires Raven to kill an idealistic Czech Minister. This is seen by the Germans as a political assassination undertaken by the Serbs and they prepare to go to war on the strength of it. Britain rearms and Sir Marcus' sales soar.

Anne, a chorus girl, becomes unwittingly involved with Raven, who is an embittered young man obsessed by his deforming hare lip. Raven tells Anne that Cholmondeley is responsible for the assassination and that he himself is wanted by the police for possessing forged notes – which had, in fact, been his payment for the killing. She discovers that Cholmondeley is the backer of her show and her attempt to expose him, thereby absolving the Serbs and preventing a major war, leads to a murder attempt from which she is rescued by Raven. Raven keeps her hostage and when her policeman fiancé tracks them down he believes they are having an affair. Saving the world has become too much for Anne and she is shocked when Raven confesses that he had, in ignorance, killed the Minister.

Raven, purified by his confession, seeks out, exposes and kills Cholmondeley and Sir Marcus. But Anne gives way to her jealous fiancé and tells him of Raven's intentions. As Raven dies from a policeman's bullet he feels a sense of betrayal, and Anne, secure in the forgiving arms of her fiancé, feels a sense of unease.

"There was no dawn that day in Nottwich. Fog lay over the city like a night sky with no stars. The air in the streets was clear. You had only to imagine that it was night. The first tram crawled out of its shed and took the steel track down towards the market. An old piece of newspaper blew up against the door of the Royal Theatre and flattened out. In the streets on the outskirts of Nottwich nearest the pits an old man plodded by with a pole tapping at the windows. The stationer's window in the High Street was full of Prayer Books and Bibles: a printed card remained among them, a relic of Armistice Day, like the old drab wreath of Haig poppies by the War Memorial: 'Look up, and swear by the slain of the war that you'll never forget.' Along the line a signal lamp winked green in the dark day and the lit carriages drew slowly in past the cemetery, the glue factory, over the wide tidy cement-lined river. A bell began to ring from the Roman Catholic cathedral. A whistle blew."

Nottingham Castle

Theatre Royal, Nottingham

DIARY

Sunday, August 25

To find a location or setting more interesting than I hoped it would be has not been uncommon on my travels. But also to have no snarling dogs, over-curious children or loquacious locals around my head, plus a good place to stay and eat, fine weather and plenty of time, *is* rare. I'm lucky if I can score six out of ten. Incredibly, almost all these factors come together on my visit to Nottingham, the 'Nottwich' of *A Gun for Sale.*

The city is remarkable for its huge chateau-esque red and yellow brick hotels and office-blocks: the work of an extraordinary architect called Watson Fothergill. His deep roofs, conical towers, elaborate weathervanes and gargoyles provide an ambience of uneasy fantasy. Little wonder Greene found Nottingham 'as haunting as Berkhamsted'. Little wonder that he used its streets and strange buildings as a powerful background for much of this memorable thriller.

"Mather's train got in at eleven that night and with Saunders he drove straight through the almost empty streets to the police station. Nottwich went to bed early; the cinemas closed at ten-thirty and a quarter of an hour later everyone had left the middle of Nottwich by tram or bus. Nottwich's only tart hung round the market place, cold and blue under her umbrella, and one or two businessmen were having a last cigar in the hall of the Metropole. The car slid on the icy road. Just before the police station Mather noticed the posters of Aladdin outside the Royal Theatre. He said to Saunders: 'My girl's in that show.' He felt proud and happy."

Graham Greene writes:
'In 1926 I spent three months in Nottingham as an apprentice sub-editor on the Journal *before joining* The Times *in London. I have happy memories of this bizarre old building with a bust of Gladstone over the entrance.'*

Old Nottingham Journal *building from Parliament Street*

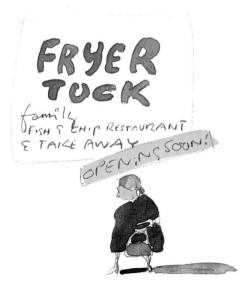

FRYER TUCK

family Fish & Chip Restaurant & Take Away

OPENING SOON!

DIARY

Monday, August 26

Draw Theatre Royal, the 'Royal Theatre' of the novel. Anne Crowder, who is involved with the hunted assassin, Raven, appears there in the pantomime *Aladdin*. A restored façade hides a modernized theatre inside. When Greene lived in Nottingham in 1926, there was also a music-hall, the Empire, next door. Unfortunately, this was demolished some years ago. As the day progresses I make a second walkabout. I search for the 'Pugin-like' *Journal* building in which the young Greene worked for three months as an apprentice journalist. This takes me through Old Market Square where a 'Medieval Fair' is in full swing. Strong regional atmosphere. Folk-musicians dress like Robin Hoods, Friar Tucks and Maid Marions. Raunchy red-nosed comedians, 'bite-bars' and satanic punks. There are unspoilt vintage pubs, the Bodega in Pelham Street and the Dog and Bear nearby are prime examples. Find and depict former *Journal* building on Lower Parliament Street. Bowled over by its bizarre bulk. The heads of Victorian Liberal statesmen still stick out like gargoyles above the entrance. 'The *Journal*,' wrote Greene in his autobiographical *A Sort of Life*, 'prided itself on its literary tradition... Sir James Barrie had once been a member of the staff.' Make good progress with the drawing as there is hardly any traffic in the street. It's the weekend of the late summer Bank Holiday.

Tuesday, August 27

Up early to depict the castle. Blackened by soot and grime when Greene lived here, it is now a pristine palace flying the Union flag. Against the rockface below is 'the oldest pub in England'.

Sense of excitement created by the bizarre ambience of the city is heightened still further by discovery of the equally Pugin-like All Saints neighbourhood. A neo-Gothic enclave of gabled redbrick houses set behind gnarled yew trees and spiky Norfolk pines. I can well imagine Raven on the run in this strange street, 'hemmed in by the redbrick walls'.

BITE BAR

Crispy Fried Onion

"All Saints Road was two rows of small neo-Gothic houses lined up as carefully as a company on parade. He stopped outside No. 14 and wondered if she were awake. She'd get a surprise in the morning; he had posted a card at Euston telling her he was putting up at the Crown, the commercial 'house'. There was a light on in the basement: the landlady was still awake. He wished he could have sent a quicker message than that card; he knew the dreariness of new lodgings, of waking to the black tea and the unfriendly face. It seemed to him that life couldn't treat her well enough."

Graham Greene writes:
'I had lodgings with my mongrel terrier in this road and perhaps in this very house while I worked on the Nottingham Journal. *It seemed natural to lodge Anne in the same spot. I always find it easier to remember than to imagine.'*

All Saints Road, Nottingham

45

[Brighton Rock]

Before Hale, a sleazy reporter involved in gang warfare, is murdered on Brighton Pier, he takes up with Ida, a loyal and good-hearted prostitute. She, intent upon avenging her friend, seeks out his murderer Pinkie, a teenage leader of a protection gang who is trying to prove his worth against experienced rivals. Pinkie, a perverted Catholic, lives by sadism and menace.

Ida fails to prevent Pinkie from courting Rose, a sixteen-year-old waitress who knows too much about Hale's death. Pinkie swallows his sexual revulsion and his disappointment at being tied to a simple doting child from his own impoverished background and marries her in order to prevent her from giving evidence against him. Rose, her devotion to Pinkie knowing no bounds, steels her Catholic soul to face eternal damnation rather than to lose Pinkie, and the more he damns his Catholic soul the more devoted she becomes.

Pinkie is horrified by the demands of his marriage, by the responsibility of evil and ambition and by Ida's relentless pursuit. He persuades Rose to agree to a suicide pact – which he intends to survive – but Rose's hypnotic state of self-destruction is broken when Ida, the police in tow, come upon the scene and Pinkie dies accidentally in the ensuing confusion.

Later Rose, calmed by a priest, goes home to play a message recorded for her by Pinkie on their wedding day. Proof of his love would show that 'there was some good . . .' The reader knows better.

"Hale knew, before he had been in Brighton three hours, that they meant to murder him. With his inky fingers and his bitten nails, his manner cynical and nervous, anybody could tell he didn't belong – belong to the early summer sun, the cool Whitsun wind off the sea, the holiday crowd. They came in by train from Victoria every five minutes, rocked down Queen's Road standing on the tops of the little local trams, stepped off in bewildered multitudes into fresh and glittering air: the new silver paint sparkled on the piers, the cream houses ran away into the west like a pale Victorian water-colour; a race in miniature motors, a band playing, flower gardens in bloom below the front, an aeroplane advertising something for the health in pale vanishing clouds across the sky.

It had seemed quite easy to Hale to be lost in Brighton. Fifty thousand people besides himself were down for the day, and for quite a while he gave himself up to the good day, drinking gins and tonics wherever his programme allowed. For he had to stick closely to a programme: from ten till eleven Queen's Road and Castle Square, from eleven till twelve the Aquarium and Palace Pier, twelve till one the front between the Old Ship and West Pier, back for lunch between one and two in any restaurant he chose round the Castle Square, and after that he had to make his way all down the parade to the West Pier and then to the station by the Hove streets. These were the limits of his absurd and widely advertised sentry-go."

Graham Greene writes:
**'All I remember of the Royal Pavilion
tavern is the blind pianist who used
to play there. My favourite resort was
the Cricketers', part of the
background to Travels with My
Aunt.'**

Castle Square, Brighton

DIARY

Friday, June 14

Drive down to Brighton, which I need hardly add is the setting of *Brighton Rock*. I'm to spend a long weekend here, staying with friends in Hove. Once the fashionable resort of Regency England, the city remains obstinately raffish despite a constant process of attrition to bring it into line. Much of its seedy Greenesian flavour has long disappeared, to the relief of the city fathers. The Metropole Hotel, the 'Cosmopolitan' of *Brighton Rock*, headquarters of the wealthy gang-leader Colleoni, has lost its flamboyant Edwardian style. 'Sherry's', the celebrated Italianate palace of pleasure in West Street, is now a vast concrete banqueting centre known as King's West. With the exception of the Cricketers' Arms and the Royal Pavilion Tavern, it is difficult to imagine the doomed Hale seeking refuge and solace in any of the tarted-up pubs, let alone leaving his Kolley Kibber cards behind on one of the tables.

Saturday, June 15

But despite these sad unfortunate casualties, much of Graham Greene's Brighton survives. The prime example being, of course, the Palace Pier. To go through its turnstiles is to enter a time capsule of the thirties. To the strains of 'Happy Days are Here Again' the young, the middle-aged and the elderly stroll by in a light-hearted mood. Giggling girls nudge one another, as they pass pimply boys. The only things missing are the batteries of hand-cranked 'What the Butler Saw' soft-porn movies.

Palace Pier, despite its tawdry pop-culture, casts a spell on all-comers. And not just courting couples, Pinkie-like teenagers and red-faced tarts. Bus-loads of bemused German tourists goggle at the anarchic jumble of comic postcards, weighing machines, one-armed bandits, chips-with-everything kiosks, candy-floss and junk-food stands, ice-cream carts and 'Hill-Billy Moonshine' stalls. Not to leave out the Electronic Stripper, Euroball and the Lace Shop. 'Coney Island,' quipped an American tourist, 'used to be like this, but not any more.'

Palace Pier side show, Brighton

"*The Boy paid his threepence and went through the turnstile. He moved rigidly past the rows of deck-chairs four deep where people were waiting for the orchestra to play. From behind he looked younger than he was in his dark thin ready-made suit a little too big for him at the hips, but when you met him face to face he looked older, the slatey eyes were touched with the annihilating eternity from which he had come and to which he went. The orchestra began to play: he felt the music as a movement in his belly: the violins wailed in his guts. He looked neither right nor left but went on.*

In the Palace of Pleasure he made his way past the peep-shows, the slot-machines and the quoits to a shooting-booth. The shelves of dolls stared down with glassy innocence, like Virgins in a church repository. The Boy looked up: chestnut ringlets, blue orbs and painted cheeks; he thought – Hail Mary . . . in the hour of our death. 'I'll have six shots,' he said."

Palace Pier, Brighton

DIARY

Sunday, June 16

Another surviving fragment is the Salvation Army Citadel just off the Steyne. Unable to believe that the battlemented thirties building still exists, I hear the familiar strains of a Salvation Army band playing their weekly stint of Sunday hymn music. I ask a bandsman the way. 'Follow us and find out!' he cries. But confronted with the commonplace reality, I change my mind about drawing it. Take my friends to supper in the old-fashioned dining-room of English's Oyster Bar in East Street. We all have large Dover soles accompanied by an excellent Pouilly-Fumé de Ladoucette.

Thursday, August 29

Second visit to Brighton. This time for the Kemp Town Races, an important location for *Brighton Rock*. Catch train from Victoria at 11.02. By 12.00 I'm in Brighton, waiting for the 44 bus to take me to the racecourse. A sunny day and the bus queue is in a buoyant mood. Arrive at track 12.30. After appalling beer and sandwich lunch, look around for some evidence of the track's dark history as a battleground for rival razor-slashing thugs from London's East End. Do not find it of course. But make sketches of the rich variety of racetrack characters; the cigar-puffing histrionic bookies, the chain-smoking touts, eccentric-looking tic-tac men and knowing runners. There's also a good range of gullible clients. After two hours, I call it a day. An equally quick return means I'm back in London watching the news on television by 18.00.

"The loud-speakers on the vans advised them whom to put their money with, and gipsy children chased a rabbit with cries across the trampled chalk. They went down into the tunnel under the course and came up into the light and the short grey grass sloping down by the bungalow houses to the sea. Old bookies' tickets rotted into the chalk: 'Barker for the Odds', a smug smiling nonconformist face printed in yellow: 'Don't Worry I Pay', and old tote tickets among the stunted plantains. They went through the wire fence into the half-crown enclosure. 'Have a glass of beer, Spicer,' the Boy said, pressing him on.
   'Why, that's good of you, Pinkie. I wouldn't mind a glass,' and while Spicer drank it by the wooden trestles, the Boy looked down the line of bookies. There was Barker and Macpherson and George Beale ('The Old Firm') and Bob Tavell of Clapton, all the familiar faces, full of blarney and fake good humour. The first two races had been run: there were long queues at the tote windows. The sun lit the white Tattersall stand across the course, and a few horses cantered by to the start. 'There goes General Burgoyne,' a man said, 'he's restless', starting off to Bob Tavell's stand to cover his bet. The bookies rubbed out and altered the odds as the horses went by, their hoofs padding like boxing gloves on the turf."

The Races

"It was a fine day for the races. People poured into Brighton by the first train. It was like Bank Holiday all over again, except that these people didn't spend their money; they harboured it. They stood packed deep on the tops of the trams rocking down to the Aquarium, they surged like some natural and irrational migration of insects up and down the front. By eleven o'clock it was impossible to get a seat on the buses going out to the course. A negro wearing a bright striped tie sat on a bench in the Pavilion garden and smoked a cigar. Some children played touch wood from seat to seat, and he called out to them hilariously, holding his cigar at arm's length with an air of pride and caution, his great teeth gleaming like an advertisement. They stopped playing and stared at him, backing slowly. He called out to them again in their own tongue, the words hollow and unformed and childish like theirs, and they eyed him uneasily and backed farther away. He put his cigar patiently back between the cushiony lips and went on smoking. A band came up the pavement through Old Steyne, a blind band playing drums and trumpets, walking in the gutter, feeling the kerb with the edge of their shoes, in Indian file. You heard the music a long way off, persisting through the rumble of the crowd, the shots of exhaust pipes, and the grinding of the buses starting uphill for the racecourse. It rang out with spirit, marched like a regiment, and you raised your eyes in expectation of the tiger skin and the twirling drumsticks and saw the pale blind eyes, like those of pit ponies, going by along the gutter."

Graham Greene writes:
'At the Brighton races, which I visited while writing the novel, I was foolish enough not to back an outsider named Brighton Rock which won at 10 to 1.'

[THE CONFIDENTIAL AGENT]

D has come to England to buy coal for the Spanish Republican government, without which they will lose the civil war which is tearing the country apart. Not only does he find London in the thirties very different from his war-torn country, but that his government's usurpers have sent an agent to England with the same mission as himself. D's success hinges upon convincing the coal magnates that he is a bona fide customer, and to do this his credentials have to be carefully guarded for the enemy will go to any length to discredit him. Inevitably the credentials are stolen, although they have been guarded – literally with her life – by a doting child-maid who worked at the Bloomsbury hotel where D is staying.

D loses the deal and it seems that the enemy will buy the coal. His desperate attempt to persuade the Nottinghamshire miners to strike rather than supply coal to a reactionary government fails, but his activities come to the notice of the Press and the dubious contract with a usurping government is cancelled.

D is taken aback when he realizes he is in love with the coal magnate's daughter. He is, after all, infected by war and suffering, widowed, beset by vengeful enemies and old enough to be the girl's father. Unknown to him the girl has organized for him to be smuggled onto a boat bound for his country and while he watches the fading lights of England he turns in surprise to find that, for better or worse, the girl has come to join him.

"It was certainly half a victory; he thought grimly that it would probably postpone his death – he would be left to an enemy bomb, instead of reaching a solution of his problems quickly in front of the cemetery wall. On the crown of the hill they came in sight of the sea. He hadn't seen it since that foggy night at Dover with the gulls crying – the limit of his mission. Far away to the right a rash of villas began; lights were coming out, and a pier crept out to sea like a centipede with an illuminated spine.

'That's Southcrawl,' Mr Forbes said. There were no ships' lights visible anywhere on the wide grey vanishing Channel. 'It's late,' Mr Forbes said with a touch of nervousness.

'Where do I go?'

'See that hotel over on the left about two miles out of Southcrawl?' They cruised slowly down the hill; it was more like a village than a hotel as they came down towards it – or, nearer comparison still, an airport: circle after circle of chromium bungalows round a central illuminated tower – fields and more bungalows. 'It's called the Lido,' Mr Forbes said. 'A new idea in popular hotels. A thousand rooms, playing fields, swimming pools . . .'"

Graham Greene writes:
*'I once visited Butlin's pleasure camp
at Clacton with my friend Edward
Ardizzone the artist, but we only
stayed one night. I disgraced myself
on the dance floor by falling down.
We found the system of "prefects"
and "houses" (Gloucester and Kent)
unsympathetic.'*

The Water Tower, Butlin's Camp, Clacton-on-Sea

53

DIARY

Tuesday, July 9

Visit Clacton-on-Sea, the 'Southcrawl' of *The Confidential Agent*. Greene visited Clacton after Billy Butlin opened one of his celebrated holiday homes here in the early thirties. Described as the 'Lido', it's the location of the final scene in the novel. Having been informed that the place has been closed for some years, I fear the worst. But eventually I do find it, lying derelict like some forgotten concentration camp of the Hitler years. Analogy doesn't stop here. Guard dogs snap and snarl inside a high iron-mesh fence topped with barbed-wire. After a security guard refuses me entry, I continue on my reconnaissance of the perimeter. There's only one person more determined than a determined woman, I reflect, and that's a determined artist.

Stop to chat with tweedy female in car-park of the nearby golf-club. After thanking God for impending demolition of that eyesore which should never have been built there in the first place, she tells me that the best view of what's left can be seen from the promenade facing the North Sea. Moments later, I gaze at silent rows of two-storied barrack-like buildings; each set off with thirties Aztec picture-palace plaster gables. Huge citadel-like water tower, lower half inscribed with inane graffiti, forms centrepiece. Grotesque beetroot-faced retirees, who look as though they refused to be liberated when the camp closed, stagger by, or absorb the warmth of the midday sun on battered deck-chairs. The scene makes a Paul Hogarth genre picture of some interest, but to whom other than myself, I can't imagine.

Russell Square Underground and Hotel Russell from Bernard Street, London

"Well, he remembered the number – 35. He was a little surprised to find that it was a hotel, though not a good hotel. The open outer door was a sure mark of its nature in every city in Europe. He took stock of his surroundings – he remembered the district very slightly. Attached to it was a haze of sentiment from his British Museum days, days of scholarship and peace and courtship. The street opened at the end into a great square – trees blackened with frost: the fantastic cupolas of a great inexpensive hotel: an advertisement for Russian baths. He went in and rang at the glass inner door. Somewhere a clock struck six."

55

DiARY

Saturday, July 13

Set out as usual, in high spirits, now tempered somewhat. I may *not*, I reflect, after all, find exactly what I expect. Although each novel differs from another in the degree of description of places, some differ more than others. This is especially true of *The Confidential Agent,* a thriller with an aura of unreality or super-reality about its locations. Greene admits to writing the novel in six weeks with the help of benzedrine. It proves hard to match the locations exactly in this case.

Today I'm deep in the Warwickshire coalfield, searching for a mining village which answers to the location described as being in the 'quiet Midlands countryside'. With the help of the National Coal Board, the nearest I can get is Baddesley Ensor and its colliery, formerly owned by Lord Dugdale who resides nearby in a huge castellated High Victorian chateau. A country seat similar to that in which our hero, D, confronts the coal-owner Lord Benditch. I ask Greene if he actually had the house, and possibly the family in mind. His answer is no. He invented it all.

The colliery itself is from the thirties, possibly earlier. Pithead gear still bears Dugdale crest. The silent atmosphere of deserted trackways and machinery (the miners are on annual summer holidays) fits mood of the novel so closely that I decide this scene should be depicted. Draw the scene from a nearby railway bridge plastered with 'Trespassers will be prosecuted' signs.

Sunday, July 21

Morning in Bloomsbury. Depict scene looking up Bernard Street, where D stays at a cheap hotel on arrival in London from a Spain embroiled in civil war. My scene looks towards Russell Square with the massive bulk of the Russell Hotel looming in the background. Between D's hotel and the Russell is Russell Square tube station. Thirties ambience is strong here. I can vouch for that as I once lived in the neighbourhood as a refugee from provincial suburbia. Takes me back to September 1938 when, during the Munich crisis, trenches were dug in London's parks and squares for air-raid precautions. I helped dig the trenches in Russell Square. The old square is lushly verdant as though nothing had ever disturbed its manicured tranquility. Only the Imperial Hotel and the sign advertising 'Russian Vapour Baths' are missing.

"The woods and meagre grass gave out as they pottered on from stop to stop. The hills become rocky; a quarry lay behind a halt and a rusting single line led out to it; a small truck lay overturned in the thorny grass. Then even the hills gave out and a long plain opened up dotted with strange erratic heaps of slag – the height of the hills behind. Short unsatisfactory grass crept up them like gas flames; miniature railways petered out, going to nowhere at all, and right beneath the artificial hills the cottages began – lines of grey stone like scars. The train no longer stopped; it rattled deeper into the shapeless plain, passing halts under every slag-heap dignified by names like Castle Crag and Mount Zion. It was like a gigantic rubbish heap into which everything had been thrown of a whole way of life – great rusting lift-shafts and black chimneys and Non-conformist chapels with slate roofs and hopeless washing darkening on the line and children carrying pails of water from common taps."

Baddesley Colliery, Warwickshire

[The Power *and the* Glory]

A poor southern Mexican state, Tabasco, under the dictatorship of Tomas Garrido Canabal, has purged all but one of its priests. An American bank robber also remains at large and the lieutenant in charge of the search for both men is passionately anti-clerical and, by contrast, feels respect for the bank robber who has only committed the secular crime of murder. The last priest, an ageing, humble, tragi-comic alcoholic with an illegitimate child, is driven from village to village. Hostages are taken and shot but the fervent peasants, although disappointed in the flawed 'whisky priest', beg for confession and shield him.

The little priest longs for the chase to end but will not give himself up; there is no bishop to guide him and he must fulfil his destiny. His path is dogged by his 'Judas', a half-caste who is ready to betray him for the reward that has been offered. He inevitably does so by leading him into a trap baited by the American bank robber who has shot his way into the hands of the lieutenant and who now lies dying but not craving confession as the priest has been led to believe. There is no-one to give the whisky priest absolution; the lieutenant gives him brandy and while he waits for his inevitable execution he feels 'only an immense disappointment because he had to go to God empty handed, with nothing done at all. It seemed to him, at that moment, that it would have been quite easy to be a saint. It would only have needed a little self-restraint and a little courage. He felt like someone who has missed happiness by seconds at an appointed place . . .'

"He stared out over the slow river: the fin of a shark moved like a periscope at the river's mouth. In the course of years several ships had stranded and they now helped to prop up the bank, the smoke-stacks leaning over like guns pointing at some distant objective across the banana trees and the swamps."

The Rio Grijalva, near the ferry for Puerto de Frontera

DIARY

Friday, April 12

After long delayed flight arrive Mexico City *en route* to recreate scenes from *The Power and the Glory*. Smog hangs over what looks like a chaotic mix of Old Spain, Belle Epoque Paris and the western United States of the thirties. Lottery ticket vendors, shoeblacks and street clowns everywhere. Browse in a bookshop. 'Don't ever mail *Playboy* magazine to Mexico', warns one American guidebook, 'it will never get there'. What will I find of Graham Greene's Mexico? Feel very Greenesian as I look gloomily out of my seventeenth floor window at the Hotel Alameda. After a shower of spring rain, the Avenida Juarez (the Conquistadores crucified Indians here) glitters with a garishly yellow aura, assuming the identity of a De Nittis cityscape of *fin-de-siècle* Paris.

Sunday, April 14

I get up early to catch the plane to Villahermosa, Greene's 'shabby capital' of the now oil-rich southern state of Tabasco; a location for *The Power and the Glory*. We rise swiftly above the vast smog-bound metropolis to a glorious spectacle of the sun illuminating an endless vista of cotton-wool clouds. A mirror-image of the landscape of Mexico itself. Breakfast follows, of orange juice, tortillas, vanilla junket, honey and excellent dark coffee. As we approach Villahermosa, the landscape becomes intensely green, interspersed with banana groves and swampy lagoons. Herons and cattle ... and oil-rigs!

Monday, April 15

I am busy drawing the Panteon Central, the huge and somewhat bizarre municipal cemetery, which Greene likened to a building estate where nobody paid attention to the architecture of the next house. Ornate tombs, some with angels perched on their rooftops, are as big as mobile homes. Within their pink or pale blue tiled interiors, tables are set with elaborate vases of exotic flowers. The entrance gateway, Egyptian in style, bears a huge sign reading 'Silencio' in

gold letters. Outside, in the nearby Calle Chatultpec, I find the wall where Catholic priests and hostages were shot, still pitted with the odd bullet-hole. Elsewhere, much of the problem of following in Graham Greene's footsteps is that of coping with the shock of the new. He had seen so much of Tabasco in 1938, a time when the present was still steeped in the past. Villahermosa, founded by the Spanish in 1598 as 'beautiful town', is now the Aberdeen or Dallas of Mexico. It's a bustling, largely rebuilt city, anxious to forget, if it ever remembered, the excesses of the ferociously anti-clerical regime of Tomas Garrido Canabal and his hard-left legion of Red Shirts.

During the early evening, just as the sun begins to go down, I begin a drawing of the Plaza de Armas, Greene's 'little plaza' where the young men and women walk round and round 'in the hot electric night, the men one way, the girls the other, never speaking

to each other'. Not like that now. Young men and women still walk round and round separately, but shout cat-calls to one another. Off-stage, cast-iron seats under shady trees accommodate lovers in the throes of heavy petting. No one gives them a second look.

Dine with a Tabascan architect who is fascinated to hear that Villahermosa is a setting for one of Greene's most important novels. He tells me of the changes that have transformed the look of the city. A whole block of picturesque buildings described by Greene around the Plaza de Armas was demolished in the seventies and the plaza itself razed. The river steamer of the type that brought the author from Puerto de Frontera is now a restaurant. The state, he tells me, is changing from an economy based on coffee, fruit and vegetables to one based on petroleum. With clean, bug-free hotels, fast-food establishments, supermarkets and elevated expressways.

Panteon Central (Central Cemetery), Villahermosa

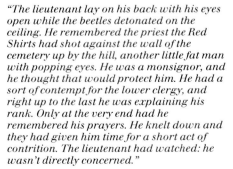

"The lieutenant lay on his back with his eyes open while the beetles detonated on the ceiling. He remembered the priest the Red Shirts had shot against the wall of the cemetery up by the hill, another little fat man with popping eyes. He was a monsignor, and he thought that would protect him. He had a sort of contempt for the lower clergy, and right up to the last he was explaining his rank. Only at the very end had he remembered his prayers. He knelt down and they had given him time for a short act of contrition. The lieutenant had watched: he wasn't directly concerned."

"Padré José went in, under the big classical gateway marked in black letters, 'Silencio', to what people used to call the garden of God."

The wall of the Central Cemetery where Catholic prisoners were shot

DIARY

Tuesday, April 16

Spend the morning and much of the afternoon drawing the huge cathedral. Completed in 1880, it was put to the torch by Canabal's Red Shirts. Now, almost a half-century later, reconstruction is nearly complete. For many years, a huge barn-like temporary structure has been used for services, to house large congregations of peasants and their families. Along one side are the customary effigies in glass cases. One contains a shrouded blue-eyed *gringo* Christ. Another, a resolute Virgin Mary holding the infant Jesus. Numerous martyrs expire with rivulets of blood streaming from savagely-inflicted wounds.

Graham Greene writes:
'In 1938 there were two families in Villahermosa with English names. The Grahams were prosperous and might have lived in a house like this. The Greenes were illiterate.'

Colonial portico in Villahermosa Old Town

Thursday, April 18

Adventurous day. I rent a car but the rental company inexplicably refuses to supply more than one-eighth of a gallon of petrol for their Mexican-built VW Beetle. So, first priority is to find a service station in heavy morning traffic. Get lost. As I hesitate momentarily at a cross-road, a large truck cuts sharply in front as I make a right turn. Rips off my front bumper. At a nearby service station bumper is fixed. Mechanics warn me to keep well clear of Tabascan truckers, they are all *vaqueros* (cowboys).

Make my way south on Route 195 to Teapa. Beyond this dusty and depressing town my ultimate destination is Tapijulapa and other villages similar to those described by Greene in *The Power and the Glory*. Countryside is enchantingly beautiful, lushly green with every kind of sub-tropical vegetation. Big banana plantations continue up to the high country where purple mountains provide a vivid setting. In the shadows of the banana groves are the flimsy tin-roofed huts of poor but friendly Indians: the *peons* who gave food and shelter to Greene's fugitive priest. As it turned out, they would also save me from a sticky end!

I can only properly depict this socially significant landscape from the edge of the shimmering highway. Behind me is an irrigation ditch full of snakes and god-knows what else. I have to work quickly but surely, as I cannot be certain that the drivers of the occasionally fast-moving trucks will spot me in time. Stupidly, I become absorbed. Suddenly, the Indian boy at my side, shouts *'Senor! Cuidado, Machina!'* – Mister! Look out! a tractor! He clutches me and we fall backwards into the ditch together, as a huge tractor, pulling five swerving skips of cornstalks roars by.

"The road went steeply downhill towards the river; on the right, where the cathedral had been, the iron swings stood empty in the hot afternoon. There was a sense of desolation everywhere, more of it than in the mountains because a lot of life had once existed here."

Graham Greene writes:
'In 1938 when I was in Villahermosa there were no spires. Garrido Canabal had left nothing of the Cathedral but a blank wall.'

Catedral del Señor de Tabasco, Villahermosa

DIARY

Friday, April 19

Drive to Puerto de Frontera, where Greene entered Tabasco from Vera Cruz. In those days, the traveller could only reach Villahermosa by river steamer from the Gulf of Mexico. The countryside here is equatorial. I drive over flattened armadilloes and giant lizards fossilized into the soft macadam of the baking highway. Tin-roofed hamlets cling to the olive-green Grijalva River. Fishermen float by in crude dug-out canoes, their women and children sell beer and melons to travellers waiting for the Frontera ferry. Despite its natural beauty, it is typical Graham Greene Country, a landscape flawed by garbage and pigs feeding off mounds of rotting melon-rinds and fish-bones.

Frontera itself is a lively town and no longer the sleepy river port it once was. In the thirties, its tiny plaza was lined with dental parlours and hair-dressing establishments. Now the municipal *parque Quintin Arrauz* is surrounded with a host of *farmacias*, *zapaterias*, *fereterias* and *librarias*. The park still retains its numerous busts of various past presidents and generals, although that of General Obregon is conspicuously absent.

Zapateria, or shoe store, Puerto de Frontera

64

"After half-an-hour they came to the hut. Made of mud and twigs, it had been set up in a minute clearing by a small farmer whom the forest must have driven out, edging in on him, an unstayable natural force which he couldn't defeat with his machete and his small fires."

Banana plantation near Teapa

[The Ministry of Fear]

Rowe, once convicted of the mercy killing of his sick wife, lives guilt-ridden and alone in blitz-torn London. When a stranger attempts to poison him in order to steal a cake he has won in mysterious circumstances at a local fete, Rowe, his interest in life reawakening, determines to find out what is going on, in spite of the cake being destroyed in an air raid.

Rowe's investigations lead to a meeting with Viennese Hilfe and his sister Anna, with whom he falls in love, and to another attempt on his life which causes temporary amnesia. When Rowe, his memory returning, finds he is in enemy hands, he escapes and contacts Prentice of the Yard. It seems that spies had microfilmed vital British plans which were to have been smuggled out in the ill-gotten cake, and now another set of plans have been stolen. The search leads Prentice and Rowe to a tailor, a jacket despatched to Hilfe, and the microfilm which is hidden in a shoulder pad. Their revelations leave behind them a trail of spies who die either by their own hand or that of an avenger.

Anna, who is not a spy, knows that Hilfe will shoot himself and she is terrified that he may fill in the tragically important gap in the memory of her beloved and vulnerable lover, the recollection of his former conviction. But Rowe already knows and, loving Anna for her compassion, pretends her brother has said nothing. Their life together will be happy but flawed by the lies to which both are pledged.

Graham Greene writes:
'*This novel was written in Sierra Leone in 1941 when the Blitz was fresh in my mind, and Bloomsbury too. The work room which I had rented in Bloomsbury did not survive the Blitz, but I had moved no further than to a flat off Gower Street, and as an air raid warden I was attached to a post in Gower Street under the School of Tropical Medicine. Bloomsbury and Guilford Street shown here suffered badly because they caught the bombs which fell short of Euston and Kings Cross. However in memory it was a pleasant time: the prospect of death enhances the enjoyment of life.*'

Within the image: WE HAVE MOVED TO; GUILFORD STREET WC1 LEADING TO MECKLENBURG SQUARE; FOR SALE; BROWNLOW MEWS W.C.1; GRENVILLE HOTEL HOUSE

"Arthur Rowe lived in Guilford Street. A bomb early in the Blitz had fallen in the middle of the street and blasted both sides, but Rowe stayed on. Houses went overnight, but he stayed. There were boards instead of glass in every room, and the doors no longer quite fitted and had to be propped at night. He had a sitting-room and a bedroom on the first floor, and he was done for by Mrs Purvis, who also stayed — because it was her house. He had taken the rooms furnished and simply hadn't bothered to make any alterations. He was like a man camping in a desert."

Guilford Street, London

67

Chancery Lane, London

"Orthotex – the Longest Established Private Inquiry Bureau in the Metropolis – still managed to survive at the unravaged end of Chancery Lane, close to a book auctioneer's, between a public house which in peace-time had been famous for its buffet and a legal bookshop. It was on the fourth floor, but there was no lift. On the first floor was a notary public, on the second floor the office of a monthly called Fitness and Freedom, and the third was a flat which nobody occupied now.

Arthur Rowe pushed open a door marked Inquiries, but there was no one there. A half-eaten sausage-roll lay in a saucer beside an open telephone directory: it might, for all one knew, have lain there for weeks. It gave the office an air of sudden abandonment, like the palaces of kings in exile where the tourist is shown the magazines yet open at the page which royalty turned before fleeing years ago. Arthur Rowe waited a minute and then explored further, trying another door."

DIARY

Sunday, May 11

Guilford Street, Bloomsbury a.m. I draw a portion of the last remaining block of eighteenth- and nineteenth-century houses: an early location of *The Ministry of Fear*. Some are cheap hotels or boarding houses. All very thirties in character. The hero, Arthur Rowe, is described as lodging with Mrs Purvis in such a house before an air raid destroys the house. He survives although later suffers from loss of memory.

Strangely enough, Greene and I were both living in the neighbourhood at the same time, he in nearby Mecklenburgh Square and myself in Guilford Street. Fortunately I had moved before the Blitz demolished much of the street, including a fine old house where I had my flat.

"Mrs Bellairs' house was a house of character; that is to say it was old and unrenovated, standing behind its little patch of dry and weedy garden among the To Let boards on the slope of Campden Hill. A piece of statuary lay back in a thin thorny hedge like a large block of pumice stone, chipped and grey with neglect, and when you rang the bell under the early Victorian portico, you seemed to hear the sound pursuing the human inhabitants into back rooms as though what was left of life had ebbed up the passages."

Campden Hill, London

DiARY

Paddington Station

"Hilfe led the way down the steps to the lavatories; there was nobody there at all – even the attendant had taken shelter. The guns cracked: they were alone with the smell of disinfectant, the greyish basins, the little notices about venereal disease."

Saturday, August 10

I'm in Campden Hill, Kensington, depicting a likely candidate for Mrs Bellairs' house: the scene of the *seance* and the murder of Cost. It's an early Victorian house set behind a high hedge: a vicarage-like respectability adds to its aura of mystery, emphasized further by a leaning street lamp.

Sunday, August 11

Much of Chancery Lane was also destroyed during the Blitz of 1940. But enough of its Greenesian element survives to make another location for the novel. The part between The Three Tuns and the corner of Carey Street is especially rich in pictorial significance. And still occupied by notary publics and small agencies who take on anything from private inquiries to typing.

Sunday, August 18

Much to the bewilderment (and suspicion) of waiting passengers, I draw the entrance to the 'Gentlemen's Toilet' at Paddington Station. One of the more depressing locations, it could easily have been the morning after the police discovered Hilfe's corpse in a lavatory cubicle.

Sunday, August 25

A further visit to Harston House. Great beeches now in full leaf join with cedars and pines to overshadow the old house. Depict the luxuriant disorder of the rear garden, dominated by a huge old cedar to capture the strangeness of the episode in which Rowe recalls scenes from his childhood here.

"The garden was of a rambling kind which should have belonged to childhood and only belonged to childish men. The apple trees were old apple trees and gave the effect of growing wild; they sprang unexpectedly up in the middle of a rose-bed, trespassed on a tennis-court, shaded the window of a little outside lavatory like a potting-shed which was used by the gardener – an old man who could always be located from far away by the sound of a scythe or the trundle of a wheelbarrow. A high red brick wall divided the flower-garden from the kitchen-garden and the orchard, but flowers and fruit could not be imprisoned by a wall. Flowers broke among the artichokes and sprang up like flames under the trees. Beyond the orchard the garden faded gradually out into paddocks and a stream and a big untidy pond with an island the size of a billiard-table."

The kitchen garden at Harston House

[THE HEART *of the* MATTER]

Scobie, a police officer working in Sierra Leone during World War II, is passed over for promotion and forced to borrow money in order to send his unpopular and unhappy wife Louise to South Africa for a long stay. The money is lent by Yusef, an unsavoury Syrian trader, who is also a diamond smuggler. Yusef blackmails Scobie into discrediting a smuggler rival and Scobie, in a spirit of self-loathing, does so. He is now committed to corruption on a small scale and each action weighs heavily on his Catholic conscience. He falls in love with a child widow who has been rescued from the sea after the sinking of a liner, but the deception he needs to practise and the pain of caring for the friendless and dependent girl take their toll.

Louise announces her imminent return and Scobie has to choose between the two women. The all-knowing Yusef puts more pressure on him and as Scobie's boy, Ali, has begun to know too much, Yusef has him murdered. The responsibility for this death is the end for Scobie. He cannot abandon either of the women; he cannot seek absolution; then in his own eyes he damns himself by taking communion, at Louise's insistence. He decides that his death is the only solution, for the women will recover if he dies but one of them must inevitably be destroyed if he lives.

The last word on his case is spoken by a priest in a rebuke to Scobie's wife, who shares his belief in damnation. 'Oh, the Church knows all the rules. But it does not know what goes on in a single human heart.'

"Wilson sat on the balcony of the Bedford Hotel with his bald pink knees thrust against the ironwork. It was Sunday and the Cathedral bell clanged for matins. On the other side of Bond Street, in the windows of the High School, sat the young negresses in dark-blue gym smocks engaged on the interminable task of trying to wave their wirespring hair. Wilson stroked his very young moustache and dreamed, waiting for his gin-and-bitters.

Sitting there, facing Bond Street, he had his face turned to the sea. His pallor showed how recently he had emerged from it into the port: so did his lack of interest in the schoolgirls opposite. He was like the lagging finger of the barometer, still pointing to Fair long after its companion has moved to Stormy. Below him the black clerks moved churchward, but their wives in brilliant afternoon dresses of blue and cerise aroused no interest in Wilson. He was alone on the balcony except for one bearded Indian in a turban who had already tried to tell his fortune: this was not the hour or the day for white men – they would be at the beach five miles away, but Wilson had no car. He felt almost intolerably lonely. On either side of the school the tin roofs sloped towards the sea, and the corrugated iron above his head clanged and clattered as a vulture alighted."

The City ('Bedford') Hotel, Freetown

"The old cotton tree, where the earliest settlers had gathered their first day on the unfriendly shore."

Graham Greene writes:
'Every day in 1942, when I went to pick up my telegrams, in a code the police couldn't read, from the police station, I would pass this tree which became to me the symbol of Freetown.'

The Freedom Tree, Freetown

DiARY

Friday, March 22

Leave for Freetown, Sierra Leone, the setting of *The Heart of the Matter*. Aspect of the old imperial past glimpsed on the plane. Groups of school children, black, brown and white, returning home for Easter, chat with nanny-like British Caledonian hostesses. I also chat, with a friendly black fellow-passenger. Tells me he has read and re-read the novel but won't commit himself to saying what he thinks of it. But he does remind me that Freetown is H-O-T *and* humid. He also warns me about 'teefing' or thieving by pickpockets and muggers.

Saturday, March 23

Awaken in the resort-like Bintomani Hotel which overlooks a Prussian-blue Atlantic. After eating breakfast begin reconnaissance of Graham Greene's Freetown. Excited to discover the City Hotel, or 'Bedford Hotel', the scene of the cockroach hunt. Also, the Cathedral of the Sacred Heart, Hill or Cape Station and the Freedom Tree. I also visit Creole Village, Maroontown and Wilberforce. Begin usual list of 'musts' and 'optional' subjects to draw, and best time to do so. Also note: tiny blood-red insect-picking birds; purple lizards with yellow heads and tails; money-changers who won't go away; the theatre-like character of street life; long lines of cars at petrol stations (there's a fuel shortage caused by the strong US dollar); hordes of tiny nimble children (bad sign for artists like me); and, last but not least, the grinding poverty.

After much-needed siesta go to work. Depict City Hotel which is still favourite watering-hole of white mining engineers on leave from diamond mines at Bo. A beggar-boy obstructs my view by performing cartwheels and splits. Won't budge until given a coin. Give him two coins. Peace reigns for a few moments, then crowd rapidly gathers around. I'm asked, why man, should I draw the crummiest hotel in Freetown? Reply that it has been made famous by celebrated English writer Graham Greene. Everyone falls about laughing.

"On his way home Scobie stopped his car outside the Catholic church and went in. It was the first Saturday of the month and he always went to confession on that day. Half a dozen old women, their hair bound like char-women's in dusters, waited their turn: a nursing sister: a private soldier with a Royal Ordnance insignia. Father Rank's voice whispered monotonously from the box."

The Catholic Church, Freetown

75

DIARY

Sunday, March 24

Up early to draw Cathedral of the Sacred Heart on Siaka Stevens Street. People stand outside to listen to magnificent chanting of hymn-singing Creole Catholics. Creoles are descendants of freed slaves from the Caribbean. When the Brits were here, they were the dominant black group, holding top jobs, as they were the only educated black minority. Both Catholic and Protestant black power waned with independence. Now Muslim tribes are ruling groups. Meanwhile, Muslim pedlar keeps kids away. 'Don't block de man's voo.' But on completion of drawing he points at my new Levi trainers. Pretend not to understand.

Monday, March 25

Quiet day up in the Hill Station drawing old colonial guesthouses built circa 1904. Hill or Cape Station is high above Freetown and was first residential area reserved for Europeans in flight from the terror of malaria. Officials lived here and commuted by railway to their offices, alighting at the picturesque Rawdon Street Station opened 1898. Hill Station today is something of a no-man's-land with poor black families living in the once stylish and prestigious 'cottages' while working as servants in nearby residences of foreign diplomats.

Tuesday, March 26

After a morning spent drawing the Sanders Street Limba Mosque, return to the hotel for lunch. Mr and Mrs Trumpet, retirees on holiday from Leek, Staffordshire, engage me in conversation.

Mr Trumpet: 'You're the artist chap?'

Without waiting for an answer, Mrs Trumpet intervenes:

' 'e dus a beet 'imself, nute sketchin' but paintin'. People lewk at 'is work and think 'eet's bin dun by Lowry.'

'The Lowry of Leek' I reply.

Settler's hut

"They had come beyond the range of the tin-roofed shacks and the decayed wooden settlers' huts; the villages they passed through were bush villages of mud and thatch: no light showed anywhere: doors were closed and shutters were up, and only a few goats' eyes watched the headlamps of the convoy."

"Scobie had been out-manoeuvred in the interminable war over housing. During his last leave he had lost his bungalow in Cape Station, the main European quarter, to a senior sanitary inspector called Fellowes, and had found himself relegated to a square two-storeyed house built originally for a Syrian trader on the flats below – a piece of reclaimed swamp which would return to swap as soon as the rains set in."

Graham Greene writes:
'This much resembles the house I occupied on the marsh flats of Freetown in 1942-3. It was empty when I arrived because it had been condemned. There was seldom less than six vultures on the roof and I suffered badly from rats and ants.'

Former colonial guesthouses on Hill Station, Freetown

DIARY

Thursday, March 28

Make drawing of famous Freedom Tree, a gigantic cottonwood, down by the Law Courts.

At dinner, the Trumpets, having seen me coming and going for days with my shoulder bag and portfolio, cannot restrain their curiosity any longer. So I tell them what I'm up to.

' 'oo, 'ow interestin' ' Mrs T says, then goes on to ask if *The Heart of the Matter* 'is a gewd reed?'

Again, before I can open my mouth, she adds that having heard about the novel, she prefers 'a light and cheerful reed.'

'Honestly,' she continues, 'd'ye like 'is bewks?'

I reply that I do, especially the entertainments, *'Brighton Rock . . . '*

'Oh yees, *Brighton Rock.* Red that one, and saw the pitcher of course. Eet wos gewd but sad like. Doan't you think they're all, like sad? The 'ero chucks 'eet in like, or dus 'imself een. My husband seys, we get enuff of that in reel life.'

Tuesday, April 2

Time to leave. Prior to departure rigorous midnight customs check at Lungi Airport. Expat with face like Clint Eastwood tells me that they're only pretending to look for diamonds. Real smuggling is done mainly by Lebanese merchants often with connivance of corrrupt officials, as in *The Heart of the Matter.*

More Greenesian characters on plane. Hard-bitten and prematurely aged Brits and Americans are going home for 'a bit of leave'. Other whites include academics, also drained by life under incessantly revolving fans and air-conditioning. Gregarious group of Americans, Australians and British officials from the World Bank wallow in first-class comfort, grateful, as we all are, to escape the arduous demands and the odoriferous poverty of Third World Africa. The incredible truth of Greene's novel remains in my thoughts for much of the flight back to England. Despite the passing of time nothing has really changed: only the masters.

Itinerant pedlar

Paul Hogarth writes:
'My intrepid driver Demba enters into spirit of outwitting the unrelentingly curious populace. Helps get me on to a roof opposite Sanders Street Limba Mosque (Scobie's boy servant, Ali, was a Limba Muslim). Built 1926, the mosque is one of the most impressive of many in Freetown. Built with money provided by Muslim diamond merchants.'

Sanders Street Limba Mosque

[The Third Man]

Rollo Martins arrives in post-war Vienna at the invitation of his friend and hero Harry Lime only to find that Lime has been killed in a hit-and-run accident. Anxious to know more, Martins seeks out the men who have been involved with Lime. British Intelligence contact him and reveal that Lime had been selling adulterated penicillin on the black market which had, when used to treat meningitis, caused death or brain damage in children. He discovers too that when Lime was 'killed' there had been three men implicated and not two as Harry's friends had 'witnessed'. He then discovers that Lime is alive, that he had faked his own death in order to distract British intelligence, and that he was himself the third man witnessing what was in fact the murder of a double agent involved in his black marketeering.

Martins has fallen in love with Lime's Hungarian girlfriend but she remains constant to Harry's memory until she learns about Harry's activities, his faked death and finally his attempt to sell her out to the Russians in order to secure his hiding place in the sewers of the Russian sector. British Intelligence use Martins as a decoy to lure Lime into the British Sector, and the ruse succeeds, for Harry does not believe that his hero-worshipper would betray him. But Martins now finds Lime grotesque and, confronting him in the sewers, shoots him.

"Martins had not realized the size of this huge snowbound park where he was making his last rendezvous with Lime. It was as if Harry had left a message for him. 'Meet me in Hyde Park', without specifying a spot between the Achilles statue and Lancaster Gate; the avenues of graves, each avenue numbered and lettered, stretched out like the spokes of an enormous wheel; they drove for a half-mile towards the west, and then turned and drove a half-mile north, turned south . . . The snow gave the great pompous family headstones an air of grotesque comedy; a toupée of snow slipped sideways over an angelic face, a saint wore a heavy white moustache, and a shako of snow tipped at a drunken angle over the bust of a superior civil servant called Wolfgang Gottmann. Even this cemetery was zoned between the Powers: the Russian zone was marked by huge tasteless statues of armed men, the French by rows of anonymous wooden crosses and a torn tired tricolour flag. Then Martins remembered that Lime was a Catholic and was unlikely to be buried in the British zone for which they had been vainly searching. So back they drove through the heart of a forest where the graves lay like wolves under the trees, winking white eyes under the gloom of the evergreens. Once from under the trees emerged a group of three men in strange eighteenth-century black and silver uniforms with three-cornered hats pushing a kind of barrow: they crossed a ride in the forest of graves and disappeared again."

Zentral Friedhof (Central Cemetery)

Graham Greene writes:
'Carol Reed chose his locations some months after I had been in Vienna. Vienna, which had been a city in ruins, changed very quickly.'

Steindlgasse

Saturday, October 5

Both the United Nations Organization (UN) and the Organization of Petroleum Exporting Countries (OPEC) have headquarters in Vienna. The effect of this has been to create an artificial famine of the more desirable hotel rooms within easy reach of the First District, the main setting of *The Third Man*. I end up with a room at the Hotel Prinz Eugen overlooking the busy Südbahnhof, the South Railway Station, which I assume will be noisy. Duly protest and the following dialogue takes place at the reception desk:

'I would prefer a quieter room . . .'

'Sir, they're *all quiet!* We 'ave invested millions and double-glazed every window. You vill 'ear nothink. Like in Charlie Chaplin movie you vill see peoples movink about. But you vill 'ear *nothink!*'

Sunday, October 6

Vienna couldn't be more different from the city Greene describes in his film story which he wrote for the director Carol Reed. The shattered palaces have long been restored to their former glory. The inner city bustles with vitality. Vienna, like London, is also a magnet for various ethnic minorities once part of the old empire: for example, Croats, Czechs, Hungarians, Serbs and Slovaks.

Depict the Josefstadt Theatre in the Eighth District, a theatre made famous between the wars by the celebrated director, Max Reinhardt. One of *The Third Man's* main characters, Harry Lime's actress girlfriend, Anna Schmidt, works here.

Vienna is essentially a city for walking in. Apart from the obviously picturesque buildings and magnificent architecture, there are the many small bread-shops, bars, cafés and small street restaurants. The bread-shops are especially fascinating in their window displays of various breads.

Some varieties: *Leinsamen Wecker, Holzknecht-laibert, Sonnenblumen, Bauernbrot, Roggenbek, Nupbrot, Winzerbrot, Schnittroggen, Hausebrot, Schweizerbrot* and *Kummel-Wecken.*

Graham Greene writes:
'A lot of the kiosks in Vienna during the four power occupation gave an entry to the sewers and the Russians for some reason refused to have them closed. I had no particular kiosk in mind.'

Old Civic Arsenal, Amhof

Josefstadt Theatre

"Martins sat on a hard chair just inside the stage door of the Josefstadt Theatre. He had sent up his card to Anna Schmidt after the matinée, marking it 'a friend of Harry's'. An arcade of little windows, with lace curtains and the lights going out one after another, showed where the artists were packing up for home, for the cup of coffee without sugar, the roll without butter to sustain them for the evening performance. It was like a little street built indoors for a film set, but even indoors it was cold, even cold to a man in a heavy overcoat, so that Martins rose and walked up and down underneath the little windows. He felt, he said, rather like a Romeo who wasn't sure of Juliet's balcony."

Monday, October 7

Spend much of the morning wandering about the Zentral Friedhof, Vienna's Central Cemetery: the location of Harry Lime's fake burial scene. I've visited many cemeteries, graveyards and mausoleums during my career as an itinerant artist. But this beats them all for sheer size and flamboyant variety. Long before Gate One, the first stone-masons' yards appear. By the time Gate Two comes into view, they have assumed the shape of a small settlement of workshops. Squads of monumental masons and sculptors are seen chipping away. Outside both entrance gates are vast flower-markets stocked with wreaths of every possible kind.

This enormous cemetery, built in 1874, contains a vast heterogeneous jumble of tombs, temples and statuary. The famous and the forgotten stand or sit, flanked by what seems to be an army of angels, mourning maidens and grief-stricken animals. Some resemble magazine illustrations of the Belle Epoque era: Schubert's tomb, for example, has a bas-relief of the composer, surrounded by a company of waltzing cherubs; while Brahms leans over his manuscript busily at work. I get some sharp looks as I draw on a chilly autumn day. The Viennese love their great cemetery and are intrigued to discover an artist making drawings of it. They watch me for a few moments with great deference but seldom stop to chat.

Spend afternoon in the more plebian Second District. Depict the Riesenrad, or Giant Ferris Wheel, in Prater Park, the location of one of the most memorable sequences in *The Third Man*. The giant wheel was built in 1897 by the British engineer Hitchins from the London firm of Basset. Traditional Greenesian amusements also flourish in the Prater: tunnels-of-love, merry-go-rounds shooting arcades, roller coasters and bumper cars. Wind up a good day with a simple supper in Bauer's Zobinger Weinstube in Drahtgasse. Waiters wear purple waistcoats and scurry about with platters of foaming *seidels* of beer.

Giant Ferris Wheel, the Prater

DiARY

Tuesday, October 8

I'm in the First District this morning, drawing the baroque splendour of the Old Arsenal of the Civic Guard in Amhof Square, where Mozart lived. Amhof is also where Harry Lime does his final disappearing act. This time behind a *plakatwand* or poster kiosk, which opens and leads down to the city's vast underground sewage system. Move on to depict another film location: the nearby Clock Museum in the Steindlgasse. Built in 1690 as Obizzi Mansion and shaped like a keyhole.

Dine at the Hotel Sacher in the Red Bar. Greene stayed here in 1948 when Vienna was divided into American, British, French and Russian zones of occupation. The Inner City was administered by each in turn. The Red Bar was then the officer's bar. Now all is crimson damask. An oval portrait of Anne Sacher gazes benignly on a scene of affluent diners, providing a *gemütlich* and reassuring note. The food is superb, the wine exceptional – a Hohenwarther Blauer Burgunder. Pianist plays 'Charmaine' and Maurice Chevalier numbers from *The Love Parade*, for example, 'Eyes of Suzette'. Head waiter looks like Crown Prince Rudolf of Mayerling fame. It is time to pay my bill. Momentary sense of panic. I discover that I do not have enough kronen to settle it. My American Express card is not acceptable. Dip into contingency funds unused since my earlier adventures in Havana. Unexpectedly find wrinkled American Express traveller's cheque for one hundred dollars. Smiles of relief all round.

"For an hour he waited, walking up and down to keep warm, inside the enclosure of the Great Wheel; the smashed Prater with its bones sticking crudely through the snow was nearly empty. One stall sold thin flat cakes like cartwheels, and the children queued with their coupons. A few courting couples would be packed together in a single car of the Wheel and revolve slowly above the city, surrounded by empty cars. As the car reached the highest point of the Wheel, the revolutions would stop for a couple of minutes and far overhead the tiny faces would press against the glass."

85

[THE END *of the* AFFAIR]

Bendrix and Sarah have been lovers for four wartime years, but Sarah will not leave her husband Henry, and Bendrix is so frightened of their love ending that sometimes he feels compelled to destroy it. Then Sarah unaccountably ends the affair and Bendrix inhabits the desert he has feared for so long.

Two years later he meets the husband who believes that Sarah is being unfaithful to him and Bendrix, equally jealous, hires a detective to investigate. He discovers that Sarah, believing that he had been killed in an air raid, had renounced their 'ordinary corrupt human love' in return for Bendrix's life and when he, who had only been stunned by a V2 explosion, reappeared, she had kept her bargain with God. But she needed to be convinced of the existence of God in order to justify the tragic sacrifice she has made, and her attempts to do this have been the cause of Henry's suspicions.

Bendrix tries to persuade Sarah to come away with him but she finds the strength to refuse. But she has neglected her health and has lost interest in living without love; her death from neglected pneumonia is an answer to her prayer for release from torment. Bendrix rails at God; God has been his rival for Sarah's love and He has won. Two small miracles, explicable rationally, might be attributed to Sarah, but Bendrix still denies the existence of God. Hate and anger protect him from the remembrance of love and the certainty of loss.

"I cannot say how many days passed. The old disturbance had returned and in that state of blackness one can no more tell the days than a blind man can notice the changes of light. Was it the seventh day or the twenty-first that I decided on my course of action? I have a vague memory now, after three years have passed, of vigils along the edge of the Common, watching their house from a distance, by the pond or under the portico of the eighteenth-century church, on the off-chance that the door would open and Sarah come down those unblasted and well-scoured steps. The right hour never struck. The rainy days were over and the nights were fine with frost, but like a ruined weather-house neither the man nor the woman came out; never again did I see Henry making across the Common after dusk."

Graham Greene writes:
'This is very like the house I occupied before the war on Clapham Common except for the colour of the bricks and the pattern on them. My house had once been occupied by Zachery Macaulay, the historian's father. The back of the house was destroyed early in the Blitz. There is a legend that the houses in this road were the work of Wren.'

The house on Clapham Common Northside

DiARY

Wednesday, July 10

After spending the morning depicting Wandsworth Prison (see *It's a Battlefield*, page 31), I devote the afternoon to drawing the handsome Queen Anne house on Northside, Clapham Common, occupied at one time by Greene himself and his family. Greene's doomed heroine Sarah of *The End of the Affair*, lives here with her civil servant husband, Henry Miles.

Saturday, August 10

London of the war years and immediately afterwards is the period of the novel. But the wet summer constantly holds me up. So, whenever the skies clear, I work at great speed. Today I am in Maiden Lane, just behind the Strand. I depict Rules Restaurant where Maurice Bendrix and Sarah Miles fall in love and leave much of their meal (and their claret) untouched. The celebrated restaurant is undergoing a face-lift. Antique furniture, fixtures and paintings are out on the pavement, guarded by security men. Am I drawing the old original Rules for the last time? No, I'm informed, it isn't changing its appearance altogether. The portraits, including Mrs Langtry's, will be restored, and the furniture re-upholstered.

Wednesday, August 15

More rain. But today I need to note the heavy fast-moving clouds discharging their moisture over Golders Green, which adds a further element of tragedy to the atmosphere. I am depicting Golders Green Crematorium, a setting in the latter part of *The End of the Affair*. The fake monastery garden-like ambience is vaguely reminiscent of a Los Angeles burial-ground. I think of the exotic 'gardens of God' in Mexico. All too easily they, too, can go over the top. But somehow those enclosures of elaborate tombstones, family vaults and bounding angels, contain the hopes and aspirations of communities. And, as such, they seem infinitely preferable to this cold and unemotional factory of death.

Sunday, October 20

I visit Clapham Common, Southside, to locate and depict Ye Olde Windmill Inn, described by Greene as the 'Pontefract Arms'. I love drawing pubs and this one is a handsome and congenial-looking hostelry, possibly dating back to Elizabethan times and later, and given a Georgian shell. At ground level, a huge and elaborate Victorian cast-iron lamp dominates windows of etched glass. Ye Olde Windmill was Greene's local when he lived on Clapham Common. So, perhaps inevitably, it also became the meeting-place of his protagonists, Bendrix and Henry Miles.

"There was no pursuit and no seduction. We left half the good steak on our plates and a third of the bottle of claret and came out into Maiden Lane with the same intention in both our minds. At exactly the same spot as before, by the doorway and the grill, we kissed. I said, 'I'm in love.'"

Graham Greene writes:
'Rules I visited first as an undergraduate in 1923 and it has been my haunt ever since, only interrupted by the war years.'

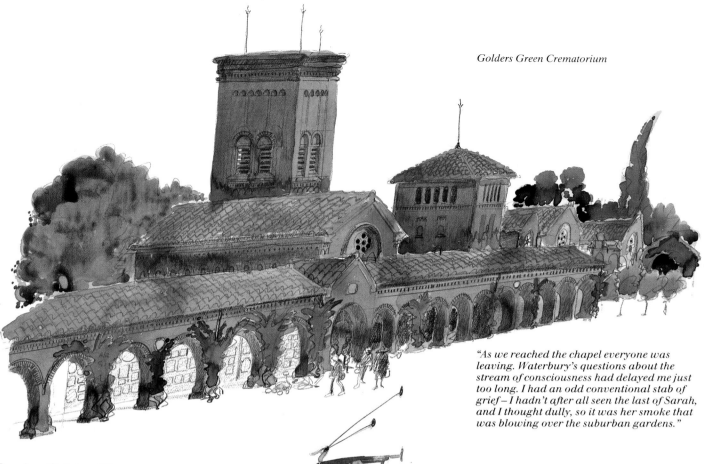

Golders Green Crematorium

"As we reached the chapel everyone was leaving. Waterbury's questions about the stream of consciousness had delayed me just too long. I had an odd conventional stab of grief – I hadn't after all seen the last of Sarah, and I thought dully, so it was her smoke that was blowing over the suburban gardens."

"Today I saw Maurice but he didn't see me. He was on his way to the Pontefract Arms, and I trailed behind him. I had spent an hour in Cedar Road – a long dragging hour trying to follow poor Richard's arguments and only getting from them a sense of inverted belief. Could anyone be so serious, so argumentative about a legend? When I understood anything at all, it was some strange fact I didn't know that hardly seemed to me to help his case. Like the evidence that there had been a man called Christ. I came out feeling tired and hopeless. I had gone to him to rid me of a superstition, but every time I went his fanaticism fixed the superstition deeper. I was helping him, but he wasn't helping me. Or was he? For an hour I had hardly thought of Maurice, but then suddenly there he was, crossing the end of the street.

I followed him all the way, keeping him in sight. So many times we had been together to the Pontefract Arms. I knew which bar he'd go to, what he'd order. Should I go in after him, I wondered, and order mine and see him turn and everything would start over again?"

Rules Restaurant, Maiden Lane

The 'Pontefract Arms', Clapham Common Southside

[THE QUIET AMERICAN]

Pyle is a quiet American from Boston – an idealistic Harvard graduate with a sense of national righteousness. He has come to work with an American economic aid mission in Saigon during the Vietnamese struggle for liberation against the French colonialists in the fifties. Fowler, a middle-aged English reporter, discovers that Pyle's real mission is to create a 'Third Force', a national democracy which, he believes, being free from Communism and the taint of colonialism, will succeed in beating the Vietminh. He appoints General Thé to lead this force, not understanding that Thé is a 'shoddy little bandit with 2,000 men and a couple of tame tigers' who will abuse Pyle's ingenuousness and his explosives.

Fowler's mistress, Phuong, leaves him and goes with Pyle who can promise her youth and marriage. Fowler is bored and irritated by this innocent and insensitive rival who not only continues to seek his friendship but has even, against Fowler's will, saved his life. After the Saigon bomb in the Place Garnier near the Continental Hotel which kills and maims innocent people, Fowler decides it is time that the blundering Pyle must be stopped and, abandoning his isolationist approach to politics, he becomes involved in the killing of Pyle by the Vietminh.

Phuong returns to Fowler. She has an oriental sense of expediency – one that the weary Fowler has learned to understand but which had always been a mystery to Pyle. Fowler's estranged wife has unexpectedly agreed to a divorce and Phuong will have her marital security at last. Everything seems to be as it was before Pyle came to Saigon, thinks Fowler; '. . . only the heart decays . . .'

"He was impregnably armoured by his good intentions and his ignorance. I left him standing in the square and went on up the rue Catinat to where the hideous pink cathedral blocked the way. Already people were flocking in: it must have been a comfort to them to be able to pray for the dead to the dead."

Cathedral of St Maria, Saigon

Caodaist Monk

"*At least once a year the Caodaists hold a festival at the Holy See in Tanyin, which lies eighty kilometres to the north-west of Saigon, to celebrate such and such a year of Liberation, or of Conquest, or even a Buddhist, Confucian or Christian festival. Caodaism was always the favourite chapter of my briefing to visitors. Caodaism, the invention of a Cochin civil servant, was a synthesis of the three religions.*"

DIARY

Tuesday, January 14

Asia looks incredibly neat and ordered after the chaos of last-visited Africa. After long night flight finally arrive in Bangkok mid-afternoon. The city's boulevards and expressways are jammed with traffic. Earthquake-proof skyscraper office blocks and enormous luxury hotels give the downtown section an American-cum-Australian look. As I enter room at my hotel, the Dusit Thani, the porter, switches on the 'nang' or television. *A Passage to India* is being shown (the awful garden party sequence). An embarrassingly poignant reminder of the colonial past. I'm here in Bangkok until January 16 when I leave for Ho Chi Minh City, formerly Saigon, and the setting of *The Quiet American*. So, I build up my strength in the pool, and tramp round the awe-inspiring interior of the Grand Palace and the equally spectacular Temple of the Emerald Buddha. It's my first visit to the Far East since a trip to China way back in the fifties; it feels good to be back in the heat and excitement of the tropics.

Thursday, January 16

I'm with a tour group for the trip to Vietnam. My companions are three genial Australians from Melbourne: Ronald and Rosemary Webster, who in their retirement are nonetheless involved with helping the Vietnamese boat people settle in Australia. Dr Gavin Dowd is a thirty-six-year-old doctor who feels a professional commitment to helping people in the Third World. We join an Air France flight *en route* to Ho Chi Minh City from Paris. The giant jet is crowded with French Vietnamese refugees from earlier troubled times, now visiting less fortunate relatives dependent on their help. One is suddenly made aware of a human tragedy as they clutch cartons and bags bulging with electronic gadgetry which can be sold for survival.

We arrive at midday and suddenly enter a very different world. Unsmiling officials in Soviet-style uniforms confront over 400 civilians from the West. Enormous piles of luggage pile up in the baggage claim area awaiting examination. We have filled in customs forms on the plane. Now more forms are handed out for completion. All foreign currency and traveller's cheques have to be declared, also personal jewellery, watches and cameras.

Two hours later, we finally emerge. We are met by a graceful young woman, Lan Hinh, who does much to help us put the experience in some sort of perspective. We clamber into a minibus and head for Ho Chi Minh City. Soon we enter the suburbs, then the city itself. Cyclists swarm around us like a cloud of bees. The city, we are told, has a population of 3.5 million and at least 2 million bicycles. Both suburbs and Saigon itself (the name is still used to designate the downtown inner city) are incredibly dilapidated – eleven years after the war ended. The gracious old French-style mansions and once splendid public buildings languish like forgotten movie-sets.

We stay at the Doc Lap, or Independence Hotel, formerly the Caravelle, where foreign correspondents congregated during the war. The hotel's Art Deco ambience, as well as its excellent French bread and coffee, heighten the feeling of having entered a time capsule of *temps perdu*. After lunch take a trishaw or *cyclo-pousse* to get my bearings. Try to locate places described by Greene in the novel. Streets are strangely devoid of vehicular traffic except for the occasional Czech bus or Soviet jeep, but are jammed with hordes of teenagers on bicycles. 'No university city in the West,' wrote Greene in the fifties, 'contains so many bicycle-owners.' There are more now, with petrol rationed at four litres a month. Street names are in Vietnamese. Place Garnier, now Lam Son Square, is the location of that premier haunt of old Saigon hands, the Continental Palace, unfortunately now reserved for senior party bureaucrats.

My trishaw driver helps me find and identify these and other places. In pidgin English he tells me his story. He is a former officer in the ARVN, the South Vietnamese Army, who survived five years in a 're-education' camp. Like many others, unable to find work because their political past, such as the Russian emigrés of the twenties, he must eke out a precarious livelihood.

"The morning Pyle arrived in the square by the Continental I had seen enough of my American colleagues of the Press, big, noisy, boyish and middle-aged, full of sour cracks against the French, who were, when all was said, fighting this war. Periodically, after an engagement had been tidily finished and the casualties removed from the scene, they would be summoned to Hanoi, nearly four hours' flight away, addressed by the Commander-in-Chief, lodged for one night in a Press Camp where they boasted that the barman was the best in Indo-China, flown over the late battlefield at a height of 3,000 feet (the limit of a heavy machine-gun's range) and then delivered safely and noisily back, like a school-treat, to the Continental Hotel in Saigon."

Paul Hogarth writes:

'The cafés and bars around the Place Garnier, now Lam Son Square, plus the Hotel Continental Palace, feature prominently in The Quiet American. The cafe at the left-hand corner was the location of the Pavillon Café, a well-known rendezvous for European and American wives and girlfriends. The cycling throng in the centre are riding down the rue Catinat, now Dong Khoi Street, the location of the Vietnamese Sûreté and, later, the CIA. In the background, silhouetted against the sky, is the 1934 Paris Exhibition style block which Fowler visits in order to buy the apartment of a returning French planter. On the right is the Continental Palace itself, where it used to be said that it was never necessary to leave: every service known to man being readily available at any time. It was outside this hotel that the bomb exploded causing many deaths.'

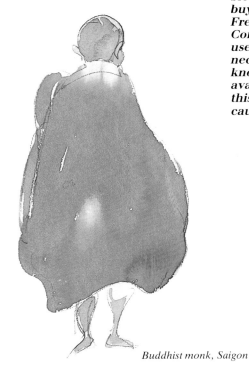

Buddhist monk, Saigon

Place Garnier, now Lam Son Square, Saigon

DIARY

Friday, January 17

A first look at Cholon, the mysterious Chinatown of old Saigon. Greene describes it as being like 'Europe in the Middle Ages'. And it still is. Streets are jammed with people, trishaws and battered trucks. Alleyways burst with streetmarkets and huge piles of miscellaneous junk. Ancient temples are sandwiched between seedy cinemas and workshops reproducing the vital parts of foreign-made motorcycles. Greene's hero, the foreign correspondent Thomas Fowler, calls on Monsieur Chou, a Chinese merchant, in Cholon. Chou's manager, the communist Heng, is a Vietminh intelligence officer. But I save that location for another day. Now I search for the celebrated dance-hall, the Grand Monde, and an extraordinary brothel known as the House of Five Hundred Girls. But I find neither. Saigon's city fathers, like those of Brighton, have demolished their primary Greenesian buildings.

Depict first subject during the afternoon, the massive French-style Saigon Cathedral of Sainte Maria (1880). Greene describes it as 'the hideous pink cathedral', yet it makes a sympathetic, almost toy-like image. In the novel, the cathedral is the venue of prayer after the bloodbath of the bicycle-bomb explosion that kills and maims many people in the nearby Place Garnier. Within minutes of unfolding my stool, my activities rapidly attract an expanding cluster of onlookers. I'm asked if I'm Russian. Get friendly smiles when I reply 'English'.

A stroll around the Place Garnier and its side streets after dinner reveals that much of the seamy side of wartime Saigon still flourishes. The homeless still sleep in the streets, while bands of small boys and waxen-faced (opium-addict) teenage girls carrying babies beg for alms. Clusters of trishaw drivers and street vendors sip tea in tiny pavement cafés illuminated with oil lamps and candles. Midnight strikes, the hour of the curfew. Streets suddenly become deserted, and remain so until 4.00 next morning.

Saturday, January 18

Accompany the Websters and Dr Dowd on a trip to My Tho, a port on the Mekong River. We travel on Highway 1 to the south-east of Ho Chi Minh City. After leaving Cholon and the straggling suburbs, we enter a vast delta of cultivated fields. Cone-hatted peasants are at work harvesting their crops. Unending ricefields glisten in the sun, mingling with brilliant green vegetable patches and sepia-hued pig farms. The landscape teems with life: here in the Mekong delta the rich silts yield at least three harvests a year.

The straight French-style highway is crowded with a constant volume of traffic. There are buses and ex-US Army trucks. Peasants jog along, carrying baskets of produce slung on bamboo shoulder poles, jostling with cyclists and trishaws for a foothold on the busy road. Here and there, villagers dry out grain on the baking macadam. Police keep watch on this ceaseless ant-like movement from wartime watch towers and village checkpoints.

At My Tho, we take a boat to visit a community of fishermen who live in seclusion on a vast island. Although it was a Vietminh and, later, a Vietcong stronghold, the fishermen managed to convince both the French and the Americans otherwise. The village became a 'Strategic Hamlet' by day and a base for guerrilla sorties at night: a maze of subterranean tunnels concealed arms and men. I decide to draw but soon abandon the idea when hordes of children suddenly surround me. If I ever complain of children anywhere else in this narrative of my adventures, I now take it all back. Vietnamese children are not only curious to the point of being over the top, they actually go and recruit others to come and see a strange bearded foreigner.

Back in Saigon, I depict the Place Garnier from peaceful seclusion of the balcony of my room at the Caravelle. Place Garnier, now Lam Son Square, was the bloody scene of a terrorist attack in the *Opération Bicyclette* campaign waged by General Thé, commander of the so-called 'Third Force' with the support of the CIA. An episode which finally prompts Fowler to expose Pyle's undercover activities (supplying plastic bombs to Thé) to the Vietminh.

Sunday, January 19

Up early. 'Le', my trishaw driver-cum-assistant is outside the Caravelle at 8.30. First, we take a look at the Quai My Tho where Monsieur Chou has his warehouse. Feel a certain let-down that the location bears little relation to Greene's description. Proceed down what appears to be an interminably long boulevard, the Boulevard de la Somme, now Boulevard Ham Nghi. This takes us into Cholon where Chou lived. I select a crowded back street as a likely setting and I send in Le to request permission to work from a balcony above. He is refused, the owner is afraid of the police. But a second request for a vantage point next door meets with approval.

After lunch we try to find the Vieux Moulin, the restaurant where Fowler dines with Pyle on the eve the the latter's assassination by the Vietminh. But we can't find the place even with the help of the neighbourhood's older inhabitants. Instead, I depict a cluster of watermen's huts perched on stilts overlooking the dark waters which flow under the Dakow Bridge. Pyle's body is found in these odoriferous waters, black with sewage and dead rats.

Watchtower, Highway 1

"In Cholon you were in a different city where work seemed to be just beginning rather than petering out with the daylight. It was like driving into a pantomine set: the long vertical Chinese signs and the bright lights and the crowd of extras led you into the wings, where everything was suddenly so much darker and quieter."

海南茶店

Tran Hung Dao Street, Cholon

DIARY

Monday, January 20

Fly to Hanoi in an almost new Soviet Tupelev of Vietnam Airlines. Again, the plane is jammed with French Vietnamese clutching packages of every kind. Seats are so close together that even my East German fellow-passenger complains. We sit bolt upright with our legs at right angles for two hours.

After the usual wait for baggage we finally get on our way. Countryside very different here, more like southern China. Less tropical vegetation. Paddy fields stretch on either side to the horizon. A straight tree-lined highway takes us to the wide expanse of the Red River which we cross over on a huge new two-tier road-bridge built with Soviet aid. Indeed, the whole atmosphere of North Vietnam generally resembles that of a Soviet puppet state. Russian jeeps, buses and trucks, all in wartime khaki, complete the picture.

Hanoi, now busy with Eastern Bloc visitors and advisors, is an interesting city, and is in much better shape than Saigon. There are just as many cyclists here but more vehicles – mostly Polish and Soviet Fiats with the occasional diplomatic Mercedes and Japanese minibus. We are taken for a quick look down 'Embassy Row' where various embassies are pointed out with pride: mostly French-style 'gingerbread' type villas sparkling with fresh paint and well-kept gardens. We pass by the downgraded Hotel Metropole and the magnificent Belle Epoque opera house.

Tuesday, January 21

A cool grey morning appropriately spent viewing the Mausoleum of Ho Chi Minh: a monolithic black marble edifice of Soviet inspiration.

We pass through the strictest security. Led by a guards officer we are ordered to march in pairs and pass into a chilly air-conditioned underground chamber. Here, Ho Chi Minh lies on a catafalque in a green-blue military uniform padded to give him a more heroic appearance. Spotlights dwell on the scene, creating an atmosphere of a late-night horror movie. Outside, a guard of honour goose-steps. One has

Rach Nghe River from Dakow Bridge

seen it all before, outside the Lenin Mausoleum in Red Square and, indeed, all other secular shrines of the Eastern Bloc.

We are shown Ho's quarters from the fifties until his death in 1969: a pleasant two-storey wooden villa of modest size facing a small lake stuffed with giant carp. A second interpreter addresses us with religious fervour. She recounts the simple habits of 'Uncle Ho', of how he eschewed the splendour and the luxury of the former Governor's Palace; preferring to live here in simplicity.

After lunch we set off to visit a collective farm in the Red River delta called 'Quiet Place' – a village of picturesque farmsteads with the dates of their construction emblazoned on their frontages. Anything but a quiet place in 1972 when B52's emptied their

bombloads, killing some seventy villagers.

Wednesday, January 22

I'm not sorry to leave. The atmosphere of suspicion and regimentation has been a depressing experience. Would Fowler, I reflect, have turned in Pyle to the tender mercies of Vietminh if he'd known what he unwittingly helped to bring about?

We arrive at the airport to begin once again the process of filling in more forms for customs and emigration before standing in line for a search of our baggage. Aboard the Thai Airways 727, westerners scramble for seats. Copies of *Time*, the *Economist* and the *Bangkok Post* vanish in a matter of seconds. We are, indeed, back in the real world again.

Graham Greene writes:
'I had never been where this picture was drawn and where Pyle's body was found for it would have been suicide in those days to cross the bridge into that part of Saigon known as Dakow after dark for it was in the hands of the Vietminh. Safety, if you could call it safety, ended with the excellent little French Restaurant Vieux Moulin, the windows barred against grenades, where Fowler waited for Pyle knowing that he would not turn up.'

" 'Well, he might have been murdered by the Vietminh. They have murdered plenty of people in Saigon. His body was found in the river by the bridge to Dakow – Vietminh territory when your police withdraw at night. Or he might have been killed by the Vietnamese Sûreté – it's been known. Perhaps they didn't like his friends. Perhaps he was killed by Caodaists because he knew General Thé.' "

"The French in those days were hanging on to the delta of the Red River, which contained Hanoi and the only northern port, Haiphong. Here most of the rice was grown, and when the harvest was ready the annual battle for the rice always began."

Red River village

Graham Greene writes:
'After a dive-bombing raid on a village held by the Vietminh the pilot took me over the Red River delta–to show me the sunset, as he explained. He dived again and blew up a boat on the river. "Why?" I asked. "I have been ordered to bomb anything alive along the river," he replied.'

97

[LOSER TAKES ALL]

An eccentric boss, known as the Gom (a figure based, Greene admits, on his friend Alexander Korda), suggests to his accountant Bertram that he takes his honeymoon in Monte Carlo where he will pick the couple up in his yacht and sail with them down the coast of Italy. But Gom forgets all about them and Bertram and his new wife, Cary, find themselves abandoned and penniless in Monte Carlo. Bertram works out an infallible system and becomes rich on the roulette tables. Soon Bertram becomes obsessed by his system and his gains, Cary bored and disillusioned. They quarrel and decide to part.

One night Bertram meets the man who holds the controlling shares in Gom's business. This man is so desperate for some ready cash on a Saturday night to play roulette and win with Bertram's system that he is ready to sell his shares to Bertram in order to satisfy his fever. Gom reappears – charming and forgetful. He reconciles the couple and promotes Bertram who, in his turn, relinquishes the controlling shares in favour of a modest life and a happy marriage.

Graham Greene writes:
'*Loser Takes All was based on an experience of my own, when I and my companion were stranded in Athens (not in Monte Carlo) by my very dear friend Alexander Korda who had promised to join us on a certain date in his boat, the Elsewhere, and had failed to turn up. It's odd how invention can affect the memory, for in my memory I placed our adventure in Monte Carlo more often than in Athens, and it was in Monte Carlo in the hotel facing the casino that later I spent two weeks working on this invention and playing every morning and evening for small stakes in the casino (I ended up only five francs to the good, not having the system invented by my character). The millionaire Dreuther has, I think, the genuine tone of voice of my friend Korda, who refused to let Alec Guinness play his part in what proved to be a very bad film of the book. I could hear his voice, as I looked out of the window at the casino, uttering these words of wisdom: "My second wife – she left me and I made the mistake of winning her back. It took me years to lose her again after that. She was a good woman. It is not easy to lose a good woman. If one must marry it is better to marry a bad woman."*'

"I put on my dressing gown and went out on to my balcony. The front of the Casino was floodlit: it looked a cross between a Balkan palace and a super-cinema with the absurd statuary sitting on the edge of the green roof looking down at the big portico and the commissionaires; everything stuck out in the white light as though projected in 3D. In the harbour the yachts were all lit up, and a rocket burst in the air over the hill of Monaco. It was so stupidly romantic I could have wept."

The Casino, Monte Carlo

Saturday, May 25

To the South of France to Nice, then on to Monte Carlo, the setting of *Loser Takes All.* Monte Carlo, now busy with tourists (who don't bother to get out of their cars) nonetheless remains the pleasure capital of the western Mediterranean. Not only is its opulent Belle Epoque fabric intact; even new buildings are going up in the same style. Greenesian characters abound: the hunters and the hunted, the winners and the losers. Well-exercised middle-aged lawyers and accountants escort tight mini-skirted young women with eyes strangely like undomesticated snakes.

Sunday, May 26

Up early to look around the Rock of Monaco as it's Whit Sunday. Locate and depict the Place de la Mairie, 'the little square at the top of the world' where Greene has Bertram, 'a conspicuously unsuccessful assistant accountant of forty', marry his beloved, Cary. I'm only just in time, by midday the narrow 'terracotta streets' are invaded by tens of thousands of tourists. Is nowhere sacred? – it's like being caught in the middle of a Cup Final crowd at Wembley Stadium.

Monday, May 27

Spend day in and around Place du Casino. The elaborate facades of the beflagged Casino de Monte Carlo and the adjacent elegantly grand Hotel de Paris, set off by a small gem-like park, constitute a unique survival from the great age of pleasure. Here, Greene spent several luxurious weeks of 1955: working by day on his novel, playing by night at the roulette table. The Casino is a mecca for gamblers of every age, creed and colour, who are absorbed and disgorged into and from its jaw-like entrance with monotonous regularity. Tourists gather like film fans at a gala preview to gape at bejewelled elderly ladies who clamber out of glittering limousines, clutching huge handbags. And, occasionally, a Gulf sheikh with robes and entourage sweeps into the Casino.

"Most nights she must have left the table a thousand francs to the good from what she had in her pocket."

Policeman at Royal Palace, Monaco

Place de la Mairie, Monaco Old Town

"*We had two minutes to spare when the furniture man helped us out on to the little square at the top of the world. To the south there was nothing higher, I suppose, before the Atlas mountains. The tall houses stuck up like cacti towards the heavy blue sky, and a narrow terracotta street came abruptly to an end at the edge of the great rock of Monaco. A Virgin in pale blue with angels blowing round her like a scarf looked across from the church opposite, and it was warm and windy and very quiet and all the roads of our life had led us to this square.*"

[Our Man *in* Havana]

This novel is a funny though sometimes sad take-off of England's Secret Intelligence Service, written by one who served in it during the War. Wormold sells vacuum cleaners in Havana. He lives with his self-willed and seductive young daughter Milly. Unable to refuse Milly's expensive whims, Wormold allows himself to be recruited as an agent of the Secret Service, but he soon realizes that he must provide something in return for the code, the microfilm, the invisible ink and his wages. He invents personas for sub-agents whose names he picks at random from the list of Country Club members and send plans of futuristic looking military installations which are really drawings of the components of one of his vacuum cleaners. SIS send Wormold a secretary, Beatrice, but she is too charmed by him to notice that things are not as they seem.

But events get out of control. He is treated seriously not only by his employers but by his enemies. One of the 'sub-agents' is murdered. Dr Hasselbacher, Wormold's solitary and eccentric confidant, has pressure put upon him to work for the enemy, and when he warns Wormold that his life is in danger, he is himself murdered. Wormold foils the attempt on his life and kills the enemy agent responsible for Hasselbacher's death with a revolver stolen from Police Chief Segura. Cynical and opportunistic Segura is angered by Wormold's refusal to give him Milly's hand in marriage and, irritated by his spurious Secret Service activity, he uses his considerable influence to have him deported.

Back in London, an embarrassment to his employers, Wormold is given the OBE and appointed to lecture to new recruits on 'How to Run a Station Abroad'.

"Passing the cathedral he gave his usual coin to the blind beggar who sat on the steps outside. Beatrice said, 'It seems almost worthwhile being blind in this sun.' The creative instinct stirred in Wormold. He said, 'You know, he's not really blind. He sees everything that goes on.'"

Catedral de la Habana (Havana Cathedral)

103

DIARY

Saturday, April 20

Villahermosa, Mexico. Leave for Mexico City, *en route* to Havana, Cuba, the setting of *Our Man in Havana*. Over the azure Caribbean, tiny islands which haven't quite made full stature, appear like partially submerged mountains with mysterious canyons and crevices.

Chaos on arrival at José Marti Airport, Havana. We have not been given entry cards to complete before arrival, so have to queue to get them. A second queue then forms to pay for hotel accommodation which has to be paid for in advance and in US dollars. Another queue forms for passport control, then another for customs. Here, a squad of square-shouldered ladies are chillingly in their element. With hair-do's like Red Army auxiliaries of World War II, they strip-search lone travellers with gusto. I'm taken for a *marinero* with my Hemingway-style beard, get a wink and only have my bags searched, although eyes momentarily narrow as my portfolio of virgin drawing paper is carefully examined.

Supposed to be met by a representative of the Union of Artists and Writers, who have kindly offered to help me identify places described by Greene in his novel. But no-one shows. Try to find cab. No-one is interested in Cuban pesos. I must pay in dollars. Eventually, I'm lucky and find an idealist. Two hours after arrival, I'm unpacking my bags in the high-ceilinged faded splendour of the Hotel Nacional.

After bracing shower in Art Deco bathroom which almost knocks me off my feet, set out to explore hotel's vast and ornate interior. And hopefully have dinner. Soon discover the place is jam-packed with Russian and East German tourists, plus groups of wide-eyed comrades from Belgium and Denmark. All, with the exception of the Danes, look as though they'd be much happier in a Butlin's Holiday Camp. The hotel's lifts or elevators are exercises in chance. Call panels are out of action, so operator cruises up and down. Stop him by shouting *Ola!* just before he whizzes by.

Dine in what was once a well-appointed restaurant called the Vedada. But now strangely reminiscent of the restaurant in Moscow's Hotel National. Local wide boys with attractive girlfriends (can they be pimps?) hang around the entrance to catch a glimpse of what they are being deprived of, and hopefully gain admittance or change western currency at the black market rate. But only hotel guests are admitted by special ID card which has to be shown at all times.

Inside the huge restaurant, the cordial and congenial atmosphere resembles a working-men's club run by an old-style branch of the Women's Institute — meaning no nonsense and get on with your meal. I order gazpacho, and grilled halibut, served with huge par-boiled new potatoes and sparkingly fresh green salad. The excellent meal restores my usual mood of idiot optimism. Cost is minimal: five pesos or £1.00 including a half-bottle of mineral water and two glasses of Bulgarian red wine.

Linger over the meal despite my hunger. The place is fascinating, like a time capsule from the fifties or earlier. Waitresses, like the ladies at customs, are dressed similarly to their Soviet counterparts. Hair swept back, grey square-shouldered jackets with party badges on large lapels, black serge mini-skirts and bare legs. Waiters on the other hand, an older age-group, cling to their original western pre-Castro gear of worn-out beige jackets with chocolate lapels and wide baggy pants with thick gold stripes. When a three-piece orchestra strikes up with 'Sunny Side of the Street', I almost expect Bing Crosby, Bob Hope and Dorothy Lamour to appear. Unfortunately, they don't, so early to bed. I can see I've much to draw here.

Sunday, April 21

The Nacional is four miles from Old Havana and transport difficult to find. As in Mexico City, buses are crowded and taxis invariably occupied, or if there are taxis not occupied, they will only accept US currency. Dip into contingency fund and wave a dollar bill: I now get around without difficulty. Arrive in Cathedral Square, where much of the action of Greene's comic novel takes place. The old city is both romantic and stylish with many fine and gracious buildings from colonial times. After decades of neglect, Old Havana is being restored at great cost with funds provided by UNESCO.

The cathedral dominates the old square. The blind beggars have been replaced by children asking for chicolets. On the left, a colonnaded *palacio* provides me with another subject, as does the Havana Club opposite – now the Museum of Colonial Art. During Greene's first visit, this handsome *palacio* was owned by the rum tycoon, Ramon Arrechavala: a favourite rendezvous of businessmen and politicos in the pre-Castro era. The famous Havana Club rum was dispensed without charge to acceptable visitors. It is in the Havana Club that Greene's hero, Wormold, plays his first match of draughts with the ubiquitous Captain Segura, both drinking the give-away daiquiri freely.

Colonial colonnade, Plaza de la Catedral

"Wormold drank his daiquiri too fast and left the Havana Club with his eyes aching. The tourists leant over the seventeenth century well; they had flung into it enough coins to have paid for their drinks twice over: they were ensuring a happy return. A woman's voice called him and he saw Beatrice standing between the pillars of the colonnade among the gourds and rattles and negro-dolls of the curio-shop."

"When Wormold arrived at his store in Lamparilla Street, Milly had not yet returned from her American convent school, and in spite of the two figures he could see through the door, the shop seemed to him empty. How empty! And so it would remain until Milly came back. He was aware whenever he entered the shop of a vacuum that had nothing to do with his cleaners."

Calle Amargura

Parque Central

DIARY

Tuesday, April 23

Begin large watercolour of cathedral which takes me all of four hours. Move on to draw the colonnade previously described and which I visualize will also make a good image. A bearded Cuban in his early forties watches me work with interest, and after I take a break, introduces himself as one Juan Moreira, fellow-artist and illustrator to boot. I am dumbfounded when he asks if I'm the English artist Pablo Ogarte, who has come to draw Graham Greene's Havana? We quickly become friends, as artists sometimes do. I am invited to his studio where he tells me that I have been expected for days! He makes telephone calls. And over lunch at the grafitti-thickened Bodeguitar de Medio – a past haunt of Hemingway's – plans are made, involving Juan's wife (a knowledgeable Graham Greene fan) and an official interpreter. We will all take a whirlwind tour of places I was unable to find, let alone identify.

Wednesday, April 24

Day of whirlwind tour and my last in Havana. Juan and interpreter Alberto arrive at Nacional promptly at 9.00. We leave in an official car for the Calle Lamparilla where Wormold and his daughter Milly live above their shop. House is identified but turns out to be in the next street, Calle Amargura. Moreover, impossible to draw as street is too narrow. I can only do so from a balcony opposite which happens to belong to – of all places – a pioneer infant school. We enter school. An exceedingly tough and hard-eyed headmistress is confronted in her den-like office decorated with posters of Lenin, Brezhnev and Castro. Permission is requested to use balcony as vantage-point. But she refuses point-blank:

'Comrades,' she barks. 'You know as well as I, the request *has* to go through the proper channels!'

The comrades exchange glances. But the mild-mannered Juan is more than equal to the occasion and embarks on a feat of persuasion. Not only am I a distinguished British artist, but I have come to Cuba especially to depict places described by Graham Greene in his celebrated novel, *Our Man in Havana*. Moreover, I shall be leaving. . .

'Ah!' she cries, 'Did you say Grayhem Grinne! Why did you not say so before!' The milling throng of bewildered red-scarfed youngsters are quickly bundled into another classroom so I can make my drawing in peace.

After hasty lunch we visit more places. We have coffee amidst the nymphs and goddesses in the cool Hispanic-Moorish interior of the Hotel Seville-Biltmore. We look in the Wonder Bar which was frequented by Dr Hasselbacher and Wormold whenever possible. Alas, its seedy interior is devoid of drink and, therefore, customers. We walk on by Sloppy Joe's to find the bar has been closed for three years. Only the name remains emblazoned on the pavement like some celebrated Turkish Baths of yesteryear. Only the Tropicana survives in the original context: the prancing gyrations of its girls watched now by Russians instead of Americans.

Thursday, April 25

Juan accompanies me to the airport at the crack of dawn. We exchange addresses and pledge contact. For him, my visit has been like a breath of fresh air. And without his help, much of Graham Greene's Havana would have remained undiscovered. It's almost as difficult to leave Cuba as it was to enter. After two hours of clearing passport control and customs, Cubana's flight 456 to Kingston, Jamaica, is ready for boarding. But just to make absolutely sure no one slips through, all boarding-passes and passports are double-checked by a uniformed officer of the Ministerio de Interiore. A security official in civilian clothes then takes over to keep an eye on every one of the fifteen passengers on the Ilyushin 62M. It's a great relief finally to get going.

Avenida de Maceo

"He walked home. The long city lay spread along the open Atlantic; waves broke over the Avenida de Maceo and misted the windscreens of cars. The pink, grey, yellow pillars of what had once been the aristocratic quarter were eroded like rocks; an ancient coat of arms, smudged and featureless, was set over the doorway of a shabby hotel, and the shutters of a night-club were varnished in bright crude colours to protect them from the wet and salt of the sea. In the west the steel skyscrapers of the new town rose higher than lighthouses into the clear February sky. It was a city to visit, not a city to live in, but it was the city where Wormold had first fallen in love and he was held to it as though to the scene of a disaster. Times gives poetry to a battlefield, and perhaps Milly resembled a little the flower on an old rampart where an attack had been repulsed with heavy loss many years ago. Women passed him in the street marked on the forehead with ashes as though they had come up into the sunlight from underground. He remembered that it was Ash Wednesday."

[A Burnt-Out Case]

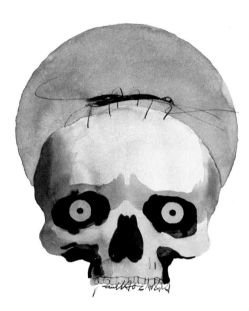

Querry, an internationally famous architect, is suffering from despair. He sees the churches he has built as monuments to his egocentricity, and his love for women as merely proof of power and sexual skill: he knows that he has become incapable of love. It is as if he has been eaten away by his success and is like the lepers of the colony to which he retreats who 'must lose everything that can be eaten away before they are cured'. He too must become a burnt-out case and then, although disfigured, he might once again experience pain or contentment.

He helps the fathers build a new hospital and his talks with the atheist leper doctor convince him of the possibility of love unconfined to God – or at least love religiously untrumpeted. His motives are constantly misconstrued by the fathers of the mission and by the Catholic colonials who want saintly models of sacrifice and selflessness to fortify their own need for pious reassurance.

Pushing his way into this retreat comes a journalist who, by sanctimoniously trivializing Querry's work at the colony in a series of articles, halts Querry's faltering transition to a life of simple contentment and exposes him to the world he needed to leave. Finally his conversion to pity for an unhappy colonial wife is tragically misunderstood by her inadequate husband. When Querry laughs at this accusation of adultery the man, misunderstanding this sign of Querry's newly rediscovered sense of tragic irony, shoots him.

"The river drew a great bow through the bush, and generations of administrators, who had tried to cut across the arc with a road from the regional capital of Luc, had been defeated by the forest and the rain. The rain formed quagmires and swelled the tributary streams until the ferries were unusable, while at long intervals, spaced like a layer of geological time, the forest dropped trees across the way. In the deep bush trees grew unnoticeably old through centuries and here and there one presently died, lying half collapsed for a while in the ropy arms of the lianas until sooner or later they gently lowered the corpse into the only space large enough to receive it, and that was the road, narrow like a coffin or a grave. There were no hearses to drag the corpse away; if it was to be removed at all it could only be by fire.

During the rains no one ever tried to use the road; a few colons in the forest would then be completely isolated unless, by bicycle, they could reach the river and camp there in a fisherman's village until a boat came. Then, when the rains were over, weeks had still to pass before the local government could spare the men to build the necessary fires and clear the road. After a few years of complete neglect the road would have disappeared completely and forever. The forest would soon convert it to a surface crawl, like the first scratches on a wall of early man, and there would remain then reptiles, insects, a few birds and primates, and perhaps the pygmoids – the only human beings in the forest who had the capacity to survive without a road."

Graham Greene writes:
'In 1959 I spent about three months in and around the leper colony of IYonda in the then Belgian Congo and this is very like the river scene I would watch every morning. It was not a depressing experience. What was depressing was writing the novel and having to live for two years with a character like Querry. I thought it would be my last novel.'

Zaire River at Mbandaka

DiARY

Monday, November 11

After long night flight of ten hours from Brussels to Zaire, finally arrive at N'djili Airport, Kinshasa, on time. Again, the strong smell of Africa greets my nostrils as I fight my way through the touts and fixers, the welcoming friends and relatives, to passport control and finally customs. Tough Belgian couple rescue me from milling throng of cab-drivers. and give me a welcome lift to the Intercontinental. Route through sprawling suburbs presents same animated spectacle of decay and poverty as Freetown, although Kinshasa does look a little more prosperous.

By afternoon, I've slept away much of my fatigue. Re-read *A Burnt-Out Case* with renewed interest. Querry makes an entry in his journal: 'I haven't enough feeling,' he writes, 'left for human beings to do anything for them out of pity.' I feel I haven't enough feeling left to continue making drawings. So that makes another burnt-out case. But knowing myself, and the ups and downs of the travel experience in far-flung climes, I hope to regain my lost enthusiasm on the morrow.

Tuesday, November 12

Have swim before checking out to catch plane to Mbandaka (formerly Cocquilhatville), the 'Luc' of the novel. With help of a pair of teenage go-betweens, pass through emigration. At first, they are puzzled by word 'artist' in my passport. Ask if I'm a *'missionaire'*. Reply that I am the guest of the Belgian fathers at IYonda. All is then well.

Plane is late. Eventually, we reach Mbandaka. Met at airport by Belgian Consul, the genial Monsieur Alfons Sonck. Route to town flanked by equatorial landscape of brilliant lush greens in vivid contrast to red laterite highway. Enter Mbandaka itself. Resembles Western ghost-town. Shops (mostly boarded-up), Art Deco houses and office-blocks in bleached pastel colours. No traffic. Everyone walks. The town is just north of the confluence of the Zaire and Ubangi Rivers. IYonda, where the *léproserie* or leper colony is sited, is just fifteen km south.

After lunch at the Consulate, M Sonck drives at breakneck speed on a straight laterite highway cut through dense bush and jungle. We pass Henry Morton Stanley's former house close to the line of the Equator. The immense and wide Zaire River lies twenty metres away: very reminiscent of the Mississippi River south of New Orleans. Here and there, close to river's edge, are fishing villages: enclaves of concrete cottages and straw-thatched huts. Large groups of naked spindly children play by roadside and watch our speeding jeep with wide-eyed wonderment.

We turn into straight drive leading to the Mission. More Art Deco buildings with huge red corrugated iron roofs. Behind are luxuriant fruit and vegetable gardens, banana groves and tall coco-palms. A quartet of kindly old nuns, or nursing sisters, greet us warmly, like out of fairy tale. My host, Father Piet Hens, appears. Small, brusque, with a complexion of pale clay. Shows me to a cell-like guest-room simply furnished with clumpy chairs and table, writing-desk and water-basin. A huge bed, covered with a mosquito-net, takes up most of the space. Pair of Douanier Rousseau-like scenes of life on Zaire River completes spartan decor. Sister Maria, a strong-featured Flemish nun in her thirties, arrives to make up my bed. Cautions me against leaving objects by window as it faces the public highway.

At dinner, Father Piet reveals himself to be tough and resourceful, with a good sense of humour. He has lived and worked here for twelve years.

'What kind of life do you lead?' he asks.

'The same as yours at the moment,' I reply, 'only I don't pray.'

He laughs at this and goes on to tell me that he knows Greene's novel well and all the locations described. Greene stayed in the same room as the one I've been given. Building had just been completed and he was the first guest. The sun sets early at 17.30. We retire at 21.00 as everyone rises at 05.30. Breakfast is at 06.30. Fall asleep to the beat of drums and incessant chanting.

Leper, Mosaka Innocent, at IYonda

"Deo Gratias was knocking on the door. Querry heard the scrape of his stump as it attempted to raise the latch. A pail of water hung on his wrist like a coat on a cloakroom knob. Querry had asked Doctor Colin before engaging him whether he suffered pain, and the doctor had reassured him, answering that mutilation was the alternative to pain."

"Querry and Doctor Colin sat on the steps of the hospital in the cool of the early day. Every pillar had its shadow and every shadow its crouching patient. Across the road the Superior stood at the altar saying Mass, for it was a Sunday morning. The church had open sides, except for a lattice of bricks to break the sun, so that Querry and Colin were able to watch the congregation cut into shapes like a jigsaw pattern, the nuns on chairs in the front row and behind them the lepers sitting on long benches raised a foot from the ground, built of stone because stone could be disinfected more thoroughly and quickly than wood."

The Hospital and Church, IYonda

111

DIARY

Wednesday, November 13

Shrill cock-crows begin a tumultuous dawn chorus of frogs and cicadas, joined by a mounting volume of chattering movement in streets of huts adjacent to Mission. It has rained for most of the night, leaving a deliciously cool morning. Father Piet and Sister Maria are at prayers as I take a shower. Breakfast follows at 06.30. At 07.30, Father Piet takes me on a tour.

IYonda, he says, is managed by Missionary Order of the Sacred Heart and covers an area of 400 square hectares. Population is 1700 men, women and children. There are 500 invalids through leprosy, plus a further 200 hard-core cases. Leprosy, he adds, is a disease of the nerves which goes for the joints (arms and legs) removing all function and feeling. Unless treatment succeeds, amputation is essential. But thanks to modern drugs, leprosy is no longer contagious. Lepers now live with their families. I'm anxious to make drawings, so Father Piet delegates an elderly leper called Antoine to keep the hordes of nimble curious children away. Antoine, confined to a wheel-chair, shows a lively interest in my drawing. He and his cronies chuckle away whenever I include a passing figure of a villager known to all.

Thursday, November 14

Visit Wendji, the setting of the palm-oil factory described in the novel. It is an establishment straight out of both Conrad and Greene. A huge and old-fashioned factory, reeking of the nostalgia of departed glory. Red and indigo butterflies flutter over derelict trucks. Huge frogs jump about in rotting barges to catch enormous insects. Snakes slither around rusting locomotives.

After torrential downpour, I accompany Father Piet on a further visit to the *léproserie*. Draw portrait of a leper who wears a peaked cap which makes him look like a jaunty jockey. He has a humorously quizzical face and reminds me very much of Deo Gracias, Querry's leper servant. His name is Mokosa Innocent and he has lived here for thirty-five years.

Graham Greene writes:
'Most of my memories of the léproserie are happy ones – the kindness of the fathers and the friendship of Dr Lechat to whom the book is dedicated. Only the nights gave unhappy memories – the cries which came from the little houses of patients, due to the pain suffered by the nerves, pain being the alternative to mutilation.'

The Léproserie at IYonda

Tomb at Otraco

DiARY

Saturday, November 15

Leave Mdbandaka today. Say my goodbyes to Father Piet and Sister Maria. I have grown very fond of them. Their devotion humbles me. Not only do they care for the needs of the afflicted. They also teach and advise a large black community to be better farmers as well as mechanics. Father Piet calls it all a stand-by operation. I shall think of him often.

On the SCIBE-Airlift flight to Kinshasa, the outside world intrudes on my reflections. Champagne corks pop. Chat with a handsome, middle-aged *colon* matron who wistfully recalls her meeting with Greene during his visit to Zaire. What did she think of *A Burnt-Out Case*?

'Just the situation as it is here,' she shrugs, adding a wry, worldly-wise smile.

Palm-oil factory at Wendji

"As they drove through the yard of the factory, among the huge boilers abandoned to rust, a smell like stale margarine lay heavily around them. A blast of hot air struck from an open doorway, and the reflection of a furnace billowed into the waning light."

115

[THE COMEDIANS]

Haiti is ruled by the ruthless Papa Doc and his secret service, the Tontons Macoute. Brown's once successful hotel is almost empty. Brown finds the body of one of Papa Doc's erring Ministers in his hotel swimming pool – the man had cut his throat in order to prevent reprisals to his family. The Tontons Macoute believe Brown is helping the opposition and their suspicions are fuelled by his friendship with Marxist Doctor Magiot, who had helped him move the minister's body so that he would not be implicated in what might have seemed to be a political murder.

Brown's life is further complicated by his complex and accident-prone love affair with Martha, the wife of a South American ambassador, and by the entrance of Jones, a confidence trickster who is often heard boasting of his wartime adventures as a commando leader. Brown is asked by Dr Magiot to persuade Jones to train a small band of guerrilla fighters. He is pleased to do so – he wants Jones out of the way because he is jealous of the rapport Jones has found with Martha's household and believes, unreasonably, that they are having an affair. Jones's bluff has been called; he dies a semi-heroic death and is celebrated as a hero by the guerrillas – his ultimate confidence trick.

Magiot is gunned down by the Tontons Macoute and Brown flees the country. Martha sadly accepts that she and her lover had not enough trust; Brown had been right when he had thought 'neither of us would ever die for love . . . we belonged to the world of comedy and not of tragedy . . .'

"I mounted the steps again to the Hotel Trianon. 'A centre of Haitian intellectual life. A luxury-hotel which caters equally for the connoisseur of good food and the lover of local customs. Try the special drinks made from the finest Haitian rum, bathe in the luxurious swimming pool, listen to the music of the Haitian drum and watch the Haitian dancers. Mingle with the elite of the Haitian intellectual life, the musicians, the poets, the painters who find at the Hotel Trianon a social centre . . .' The tourist brochure had been nearly true once."

Graham Greene writes:
'The Oloffson Hotel always reminded me of one of the bizarre houses drawn by Addams in The New Yorker **and I believe that he had spent two honeymoons there. I occupied the John Gielgud suite (far right, under the conical turret). This gave me an unrivalled vantage-point to observe the goings-on of my fellow-guests who comprised 'Mr and Mrs Smith' and the Italian manager of the Casino – no-one else. On my last day the manager was fetched from his breakfast by two Tontons Macoute – the Casino was losing money.**

Grand Hotel Oloffson

Henri Christophe Statue, Place des Armes, Port-au-Prince

DIARY

Thursday, April 25

En route to Haiti via Kingston, Jamaica, from Havana, Cuba. Horror of all possible horrors. My fear that one day on my travels I would lose my drawings finally materializes. My large wardrobe bag with portfolio of drawings from Mexico and Cuba inside fails to turn up on the baggage carousel at Kingston airport. Air Jamaica and Cubana will do their best to trace the missing bag as I leave for Haiti tomorrow. Check in at the New Kingston Hotel: I have less than an hour to buy toothbrush, replacement sketchbook, pencils and brushes.

Still no news of the bag. At dinner console myself by sampling Jamaican wine which is unexpectedly excellent. Monterey white, a medium dry wine with pleasantly fruity bouquet reminiscent of a Chenin Blanc grape, accompanies a fish course. I follow this up with a half-bottle of Montpelier Red, a light Burgundy with the astringent flavour of a mature Barolo. But despite this attempt to drown my sorrows, spend a sleepless night, worrying about the fate of my drawings. At least I have my working sketchbook in which I invariably make rough compositional notes of how and when to draw subjects. I might be able to re-draw from such notes or photographs. Then, with a sinking heart, realize that some I can never re-create. I think of Victorian Special Artist, Melton Prior, who actually wept on discovering the loss of an irreplaceable sketchbook during the Zulu War, containing his sketches of the whole campaign.

'"You have heard,' Doctor Magiot said, 'of the Emperor Christophe?'
'Of course.'
'Those days could return very easily. More cruelly perhaps and certainly more ignobly. God save us from a little Christophe.'"

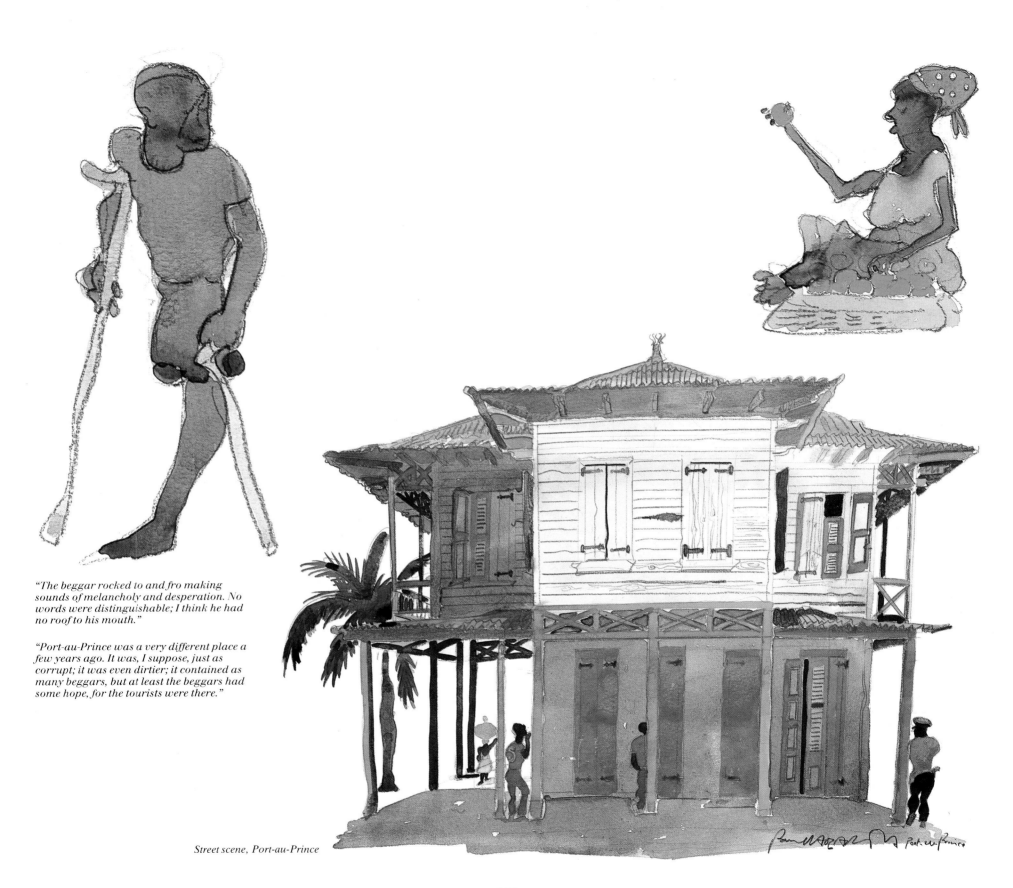

"The beggar rocked to and fro making sounds of melancholy and desperation. No words were distinguishable; I think he had no roof to his mouth."

"Port-au-Prince was a very different place a few years ago. It was, I suppose, just as corrupt; it was even dirtier; it contained as many beggars, but at least the beggars had some hope, for the tourists were there."

Street scene, Port-au-Prince

DIARY

Friday, April 26

An early morning telephone call to a Carlos Rameirez of Cubana brings a breezy response. He is confident the bag will turn up in three or four days. Thinks it may have gone on an earlier Aeroflot flight to Lima. I fervently hope so.

Arrive at Jean-Jacques Duvalier Airport, Port-au-Prince. Undergo fearsome customs search of one remaining bag. Thank my lucky stars I didn't bring copy of *The Comedians*: 'the only one of my books,' Greene told Marie-Françoise Allain, 'which I began with the intention of expressing a point of view ... to fight the horror of Papa Doc's dictatorship'. Papa Doc died in 1971, but regime of his president-for-life successor, Bébé Doc Duvalier, as recent events have revealed, wasn't all that different. Copies of *The Comedians* are still confiscated on entry: much to the utter bewilderment of unsuspecting American tourists who think it the obvious choice of holiday reading matter.

After finally clearing customs, I'm confronted by a daunting throng of bellowing touts. Gravitate towards the relatively honest countenance of cab-driver named Antoine. We career through ramshackle suburbs of shanty towns to eventually enter the serene *quartier* of Pacot where my hotel, the Grand Hotel Oloffson, is situated. Described by Greene as the 'Trianon', the hotel exceeds all expectations. It is a magnificent gingerbread style mansion set in grounds luxuriant with royal palms, huge magnolia bushes, mango and banana trees. Great massed growths of bougainvillaea hang like mattresses over fretwork balconies. My chambre overlooks a softly stirring thicket of palms set against the distant city below. Beyond, the Caribbean twinkles like a jewelled crown.

Two-thirds of the hotel's thirty-odd rooms are reserved each year by a devoted élite of artists, writers and showbiz folks, who find the hotel's low-key informality a relaxing haven. It is not so much a hotel as a super-pension, the kind one hears flourished in the thirties: a unique survivor in this age of package travel.

Rooms and suites are named after celebrated visitors who may, or may not, have actually occupied them, although all have stayed at the hotel. There are chambres and studios named after Marlon Brando, Graham Greene, Oliver Messel, Mick Jagger, Budd Schulberg and Michael York. There are suites named after Charles Addams (not surprisingly), Anne Bancroft and Lillian Hellman. Most memorable is the Sir John Gielgud Suite which Greene himself occupied. Its main room is unusual in that it boasts a banister for a wall on two sides, permitting the guest the rare experience of sleeping or entertaining under the stars.

Saturday, April 27

Early morning swim in the Oloffson pool. It is here that our hero Brown finds the corpse of a former Minister, the Secretary of Social Welfare, who, anticipating arrest by the dreaded Tontons Macoute, commits suicide. Spend rest of day in Port-au-Prince. Depict the Henri Christophe statue in Place des Armes. The statue is focal point for students who peruse English textbooks. Like Oxford and Cambridge, the town abounds in English language schools: their premises being usually picturesque gingerbread style mansions west of the Square of Heroes, along the Avenue Lamartinière. Christophe, who was the model for Eugene O'Neill's *Emperor Jones*, was one of Toussaint L'Ouverture's generals in the armed struggle of black slaves to free themselves from Spanish and French rule (1791-1825).

Haitians watch my activities with myopic interest. But they sometimes have disconcerting habit of jabbing a begrimed forefinger on drawings to make a point absolutely clear. Taxi-touts are greatest nuisance and won't take no for an answer until you've actually made other arrangements. Students are more congenial company. They like to practise their English and often they are helpful. One alerts me with a whistle and a gesture to the danger of walking too near the National Palace, the presidential residence. '*Man*,' he hisses, 'you can't sketch dat place,' holding an imaginary pistol to his head. A gun barrel glistens dully in the embrasure of a nearby concrete sentry post as if to make sure I've got the message.

GRAND VUE
Fruits de MER

*"He [Dr Magiot] lived on the lower slopes of
Pétionville in a house of three storeys like a
miniature version of my own hotel with its
tower and its lace-work balconies."*

Gingerbread mansion in the Rue Teffo, Port-au-Prince

121

DIARY

Sunday, April 28

Spend gruelling day in the Iron Market neighbourhood. The market building itself is a magnificent cast-iron structure, said to have been designed by Eiffel. Around the huge market scores of artisan workshops turn out vast quantities of tourist souvenirs.

Money-changers and pickpockets thrive, as often as not preying on their own people, as well as the adventurous tourist. Not a place to visit without a tough and friendly guide. The market is a magnet for thousands of hapless women and children who camp out in adjacent streets amidst piles of rotting refuse; performing all private functions in public.

Back at the Oloffson, the bar attracts a colourful ensemble of guests and expats, as it does every evening. They are mostly Americans, who at this time of the year are mainly journalists or young business-couples. A sprinkling of Haitian art-dealers, go-betweens and fixers enliven the proceedings with their genial hustling of services. Among them the spritely Aubelin Jolicoeur, represented as the journalist 'Petit Pierre' in *The Comedians*. Darting hither and thither and anxious to know everyone's business, so he can presumably report anything of interest to his masters the secret police. Readily appreciate why Greene left the luxury of his previous hotel, El Rancho, for such a novelist's paradise.

Monday, April 29

Red-letter day. Place call to Kingston, Jamaica. Eventually get through to Carlos Rameirez who informs me that my bag has been found in Panama! Moreover, it will arrive shortly on an Air Jamaica flight at midday! Hasten to the airport to be faced with the chastening spectacle of a great heap of lost and battered bags – looking not unlike Dali's celebrated desert landscape with melting pocket-watches hanging from dead trees. Suddenly possessed by a sentiment of devout gratitude, I kneel to kiss my bag on the baking tarmac.

Tuesday, April 30

Partly because it's off-season and partly because of the prevailing impression that AIDS originated in Haiti, business is bad. There are few tourists. Guides and cab-drivers (usually the same person) approach guests at breakfast to ask their plans. 'Bonjour, Papa Ogarte,' cries the one who has adopted me. Papa Doc Hogarth, I reflect bitterly. But comfort myself with the thought that Hemingway was also dubbed 'Papa' in the Caribbean. I get on with drawing the quirky grandeur of the Oloffson for the rest of the morning. Haiti is uniquely rich in Victorian domestic architecture, and the hotel is a prime example. It was designed by a French architect, Monsieur Brunet, and built in 1887 for Demosthenes Sam, son of then President of Haiti, Tiresias Simon Sam.

Wednesday, May 1

Almost as big a relief to leave Haiti as it was Cuba. A smooth flight to Miami where I take a late night flight to Buenos Aires. But more of that later.

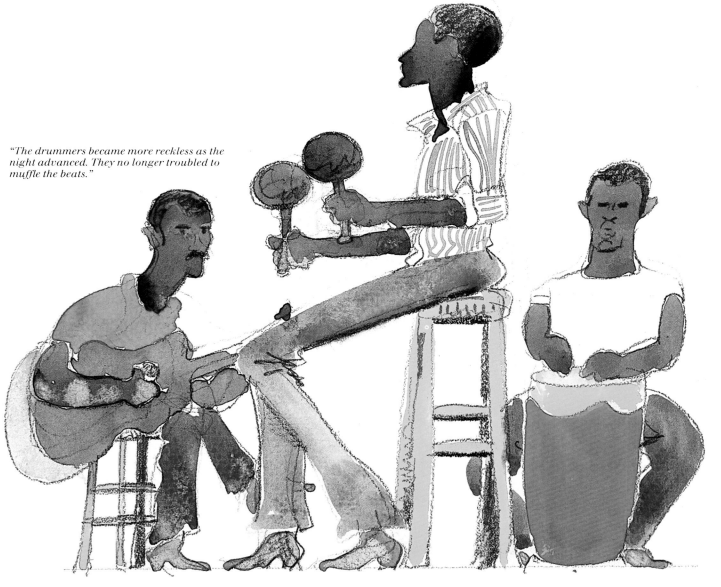

"The drummers became more reckless as the night advanced. They no longer troubled to muffle the beats."

"It was an area of small houses and abandoned gardens. Here had lived in the old days the vain and the insufficiently successful; they were on the road to Pétionville, but they had not quite arrived there; the advocate who picked up the unconsidered cases, the failed astrologer and the doctor who preferred his rum to his patients."

Gingerbread mansions in the Avenue Lamartinière, Port-au-Prince

[MAY WE BORROW YOUR HUSBAND?]

In the first story in this volume a middle-aged writer wintering in a hotel at Antibes observes his fellow guests. A homosexual couple, vicious, self-conscious and amusing, are salaciously observing newly-wed Peter whose wedding nights with his wife Poopy seem to be unsuccessful. The homosexual couple move in on the unsuspecting pair and seduce Peter. Poopy, young, beautiful and unaware, has been using the writer as confidant and comforter and he, who has hopelessly and nostalgically fallen in love with her, finds it impossible to tell her that Peter's impotence is due to his latent homosexuality and not to her lack of charm. Once the younger of the homosexuals has assured Peter of his virility he is able to act well enough to allay Poopy's fears and the writer sadly watches the girl innocently falling in with plans which will ensure that when she returns to England she will experience the pain of a *ménage à trois*.

Graham Greene writes:
'*Since 1959 the restaurant Felix au Port has been my "home from home". No restaurant can compete with it for the simplicity and excellence of its cooking and for the friendliness of its welcome. Dining alone I found short stories served to me with my meal – at least two found their way into print in the volume* May We Borrow Your Husband?'

Chez Felix au Port, Antibes

chez felix, Antibes

Auberge Provençale, Place Nationale, Antibes

"It was the time of year I liked best, when Juan les Pins becomes as squalid as a closed fun-fair with Lunar Park boarded up and cards marked Fermeture Annuelle outside the Pam-Pam and Maxim's, and the Concours International Amateur de Striptease at the Vieux Colombiers is over for another season. Then Antibes comes into its own as a small country town with the Auberge de Provence full of local people and old men sit indoors drinking beer or pastis at the glacier in the Place de Gaulle. The small garden, which forms a roundabout on the ramparts, looks a little sad with the short stout palms bowing their brown fronds; the sun in the morning shines without any glare, and the few white sails move gently on the unblinding sea.

You can always trust the English to stay on longer than others into the autumn. We have a blind faith in the southern sun and we are taken by surprise when the wind blows icily over the Mediterranean. Then a bickering war develops with the hotel-keeper over the heating on the third floor, and the tiles strike cold underfoot."

Place Nationale, Antibes

DIARY

Tuesday, May 28

After completing my work on *Loser Takes All* in Monte Carlo and Monaco Old Town (see page 100), I continue on to Antibes, the setting of *May We Borrow Your Husband?* Greene has invited me to join him for dinner. Despite our long association, we have never actually met one another. He greets me with unexpected warmth and I'm introduced to Yvonne, his lively friend and companion of many years. All goes well and over drinks both chuckle at my stories of adventures in Graham Greene Country. My watercolours of Sierra Leone, Mexico and Cuba are examined with intense interest and both are generously complimentary. Am moved to ask if he accepts Paul Theroux's definition of travel as an exercise in optimism. Greene replies, 'Not in my case,' with deadpan irony.

After a pleasant dinner at Chez Felix au Port, we walk about the Old Town. I see now how much he is moved by buildings and neighbourhoods. We walk past the cathedral: I felt he especially wanted me to see the superb front against the background of choral music being played within. A moving spiritual element set firmly in a contemporary or historical context. We are to meet again in the morning.

Wednesday, May 29

Greene takes me on a tour of Antibes. Has many useful suggestions of locations and not only for *May We Borrow Your Husband?* Yvonne joins us for lunch, and again we eat at Chez Felix au Port. She provokes a discussion on what makes artists and writers tick. I suggest that all art is perhaps an elaborate form of self-entertainment designed chiefly to keep boredom away. Greene nods in agreement. I am asked about the difficulties and pressures of having to evolve images to a deadline of travel dates. I reply that my ability to achieve this may be something to do with the extra energy generated by the shock of things previously unseen plus the excitement of working against the clock. But I find it difficult to add that it's simply that I'm the kind of artist we've always had lots of in England. The artist who is primarily a reporter, a commentator on the 'moral landscapes' of our time. Greene understands, and recalls writing a novel in six weeks just to ensure his family had enough to survive.

Yvonne warms to such talk and introduces another line of discussion. Would each of us, given a second chance, be, in my case, an artist, and, in Graham's case, a writer? The maestro replies that he would prefer to be a good secondhand bookseller and bookfinder. He would attend auctions, especially those at stately homes and country houses where he would look for rare editions but only for special clients. I say that I'd like to own a modest but venerable vineyard plus attendant *château* or *finca*, and make good wine, assisted by two, possibly three, faithful retainers.

Yvonne then concludes from our confessions that we are both dependent on others, possibly because of the enforced loneliness of our respective professions.

"Then one evening I found her in tears outside the Musée Grimaldi. I had been fetching my papers, and, as my habit was, I made a round by the Place Nationale with the pillar erected in 1819 to celebrate – a remarkable paradox – the loyalty of Antibes to the monarchy and her resistance to les Troupes Etrangères, *who were seeking to re-establish the monarchy. Then, according to rule, I went on by the market and the old port and Lou-Lou's restaurant up the ramp towards the cathedral and the Musée, and there in the grey evening light, before the street-lamps came on, I found her crying under the cliff of the château."*

Graham Greene writes:
'The statues by Giacometti outside the Musée Picasso remind me of my only meeting with the artist in his Paris studio where he showed me the origin of many of his works – the Roman statuettes a few inches high fished out of the Seine.'

Château Grimaldi, Antibes

DIARY

Le Pétanque, Antibes

Thursday, May 30

Antibes has great character: it possesses the low-profile tranquility of a small town yet remains essentially a fishing port. I can understand why Greene spends so much of his year here and has done for the past twenty years or so.

This is my last day and I tackle various subjects with desperate but relaxed vigour. By midday I have two completed: Chez Felix au Port through the Main Gate from the Old Port, plus Château Grimaldi. Look inside Chez Felix to find the maestro at lunch, reading the *Spectator* (Jeff Bernard's column, 'Low Life', gets early and usually appreciative attention). I invite Greene to dine with me at the Auberge Provençale. Again, it proves to be a congenial occasion.

"She said that she had seen nothing of Antibes but the ramparts and the beach and the lighthouse, so I walked her around the small narrow backstreets where the washing hung out of the windows as in Naples and there were glimpses of small rooms overflowing with children and grandchildren; stone scrolls were carved over the ancient doorways of what had once been noblemen's houses; the pavements were blocked by barrels of wine and the streets by children playing at ball. In a low room on a ground floor a man sat painting the horrible ceramics which would later go to Vallauris to be sold to tourists in Picasso's old stamping-ground – spotted pink frogs and mauve fish and pigs with slits for coins."

The Great Vine, Rue Saint-Esprit, Antibes

[TRAVELS *with* MY AUNT]

Septuagenarian Aunt Augusta spirits retired bank manager Pulling from his safe and mundane life and takes him on her travels. He discovers that she enjoys smuggling, younger lovers and brushes with Interpol; that she has inhabited the underworld and many European hotel bedrooms for most of her life. Travel and excitement, she says, keep the walls of death at bay. Pulling begins to enjoy himself; his dahlias, his domestic routine and his improbable fiancée become insignificant.

After his first taste of adventure, Pulling hears nothing from his aunt until he is summoned to Paraguay where he finds that she has saved her favourite lover Visconti from danger and penury and they have plans to set up a highly lucrative smuggling venture together. But money is needed to pay off the CIA who are interested in Visconti's nefarious wartime and post-wartime deals in Italy. This is provided by Pulling who has, at his Aunt's behest, inadvertently smuggled an undetectable forgery of a drawing by Leonardo da Vinci into Paraguay. This ill-gotten gain is sold to the US government through the CIA and indemnity secured for the happy couple.

Pulling is now completely hooked by the twilight of the underworld and he is not surprised when Aunt Augusta confirms his suspicions that she is his mother. She had told him earlier that her sister, his late mother, had adopted him and he now understands why Augusta speaks of his father with nostalgic tenderness. She and Visconti get married and Pulling agrees to stay with them in Asunción and help them run the family 'import/export' business.

"Outside the gates of the Ville Haute there was a plaque commemorating the death of a 'Hero of the Resistance'. 'The dead of an army,' my aunt said, 'become automatically heroes like the dead of the Church become martyrs. I wonder about this man St Thomas. I would have thought he was very lucky to die in Orvieto rather than in Hereford. A small civilized place even today with a far, far better climate and an excellent restaurant in the Via Garibaldi.'
'Are you really a Roman Catholic?' I asked my aunt with interest. She replied promptly and seriously, 'Yes, my dear, only I just don't believe in all the things they believe in.'"

Porte des Dunes, Boulogne-sur-Mer

The Cricketers', Brighton

"We had dinner that night at the Cricketers', a small public house nearly opposite a second-hand bookseller, where I saw a complete set of Thackeray for sale at a very reasonable price . . ."

When I wrote that we had dinner at the Cricketers', it would have been more correct to say we ate a substantial snack. There were baskets of warm sausages on the bar, and we helped ourselves and washed the sausages down with draught Guinness. I was surprised by the number of glasses my aunt could put down and feared a little for her blood pressure."

DIARY

Saturday, October 12

Greene's novels are usually set in a single country or city. In *Travels With My Aunt*, however, the reader is taken back and forth on a series of world-wide adventures. After Brighton, Buenos Aires and Asunción, I'm now in Boulogne still following the trail of Henry Pulling and his Aunt Augusta.

Boulogne-sur-Mer is full of Brits on weekend shopping sprees, hell-bent, it appears, on buying up half the town's food and wine. Despite the pink wallpaper and fake water-colours of the Hôtel de Londres, I'm lucky to get a room at all. Brits have always liked the town: 5,000 of them lived here in the eighteenth century. Among them political refugees like John Wilkes as well as duellists running away from their misdeeds. Apart from the weekend shoppers, the old town is a Mecca for hundreds of youngish, newly-married middle-class couples who look very pleased with themselves as they tuck into a good French meal in the restaurants of the Ville Haute, or Upper Town. I follow their example, after a quick reconnaissance of its pictorial possibilities.

"To find my father's grave in the enormous grey cemetery would have been like finding an individual house without a street number in Camden Town. The noise of trains came up from below the hill and the smoke of coal fires from the high town blew across the maze of graves. A man from a little square house, which was like a tomb itself, offered to conduct us. I had brought a wreath of flowers, though my aunt thought my gesture a little exaggerated. 'They will be very conspicuous,' she said. 'The French believe in remembering the dead once a year on the Feast of All Souls. It is tidy and convenient like Communion at Easter,' and it is true that I saw few flowers, even immortelles, among the angels, the cherubs, the bust of a bald man like a lycée professor, and the huge tomb, which apparently contained La Famille Flageollet. An English inscription on one monument caught my eye: 'In loving memory of my devoted son Edward Rhodes Robinson who died in Bombay where he is buried', but there was nothing English about his pyramid. Surely my father would have preferred an English graveyard of lichened stones with worn-out inscriptions and tags of pious verse to these shiny black made-to-last slabs which no Boulogne weather could ever erode, all with the same headlines, like copies of the same newspaper: 'À la mémoire', 'Ici repose le corps . . .' Except for a small elderly woman in black who stood with bowed head at the end of a long aisle like the solitary visitor in a provincial museum there seemed no one but ourselves in the whole heartless place.

'Je me suis trompé,' our conductor said, turning sharply on his heel, and he led us back towards the grave where the old woman stood, apparently in prayer.

'How odd! There seems to be another mourner,' Aunt Augusta said, and sure enough, on the slab of marble lay a wreath twice as large as mine made of flowers twice as expensive from the hot-houses of the south. I laid my own beside it. The headlines were hidden: there was only part of my father's name sticking out like an exclamation: '. . . chard Pulling', and a date, October 2, 1923."

The Cemetery, Boulogne-sur-Mer

Hotel St James & Albany, Paris

"My aunt had booked rooms in the St James & Albany, an old-fashioned double hotel, of which one half, the Albany, faces the Rue de Rivoli and the other, the St James, the Rue Saint-Honoré. Between the two hotels lies the shared territory of a small garden, and on the garden front of the St James I noticed a plaque which tells a visitor that here La Fayette signed some treaty or celebrated his return from the American revolution, I forget which."

Graham Greene writes:
'The last time that I stayed in the St James & Albany, my favourite Paris hotel, proved unfortunate but memorable. Neither lift nor telephone worked and I was kept awake at 01.00 in the morning by an electric drill in the Rue de Rivoli. I silenced the drill by throwing all the electric bulbs in my room in the direction of the noise. It was at the time of the Algerian War and the explosions brought silence and police cars, so I fell asleep happily in the quiet that followed. I left next day and can only wonder how they explained to my successor the absence of all bulbs in his room.'

DIARY

Sunday, October 13

Depict the Porte de Dunes, the magnificently preserved entrance gateway to the Upper, or Old Town. I follow this up with a drawing of the strangely evocative grey cemetery where Henry Pulling not only discovers his father's grave but meets his companion, Miss Paterson. Spend second night in Hôtel de Londres prior to merciful early morning departure for Paris. But now more inclined to accept pink wallpaper and fake water-colours. You could call it the artistic temperament. I would say it's more like 'just one more night'.

Wednesday, October 16

Paris. I'm trying my level best to draw the entrance portico of the Hotel St James & Albany in the Rue St Honoré. It isn't at all easy so make it a small drawing. The narrow old street is jammed with morning traffic which, of course, blocks off my view from time to time. There's double parking too, and large bulky trucks constantly deliver supplies to the many restaurants and cafés. To add to the confusion, tour-buses enter the street, belching fumes. On such occasions, I think of the peaceful lot of Edward Lear and other chroniclers of the Grand Tour.

The house at Asunción

"It was an enormous house with a great untidy lawn which ended in a dark green fuzz of trees, a small wood of banana, orange, lemon, grapefruit, lapacho. On the two sides visible to me through the gates wide stone steps led up to separate entrances. The walls were blotched with lichen and were four stories high.

'It's a millionaire's house,' I said.

'You jus wait,' Wordsworth replied.

The iron gates were rusty and padlocked. Worn pineapples were carved on the gateposts, but the gates, draped with barbed wire, had lost their dignity. A millionaire may once have lived there, I thought, but no longer.

Wordsworth led me round the corner of the street and we approached the house from the back through a little door which he locked behind him and through the grove of sweet-smelling trees and bushes. 'Hi!' he called to the great square block of stone, 'hi!' and got no response. The house in its solidity and its silence reminded me of the great family tombs in the cemetery at Boulogne. This was a journey's end too.

'Your auntie she got a bit deaf,' Wordsworth said, 'she no young no more, no more.' He spoke regretfully, as though he had known her as a girl, and yet she had been over seventy when she picked him up outside the Grenada Palace. We went up one flight of stone steps and into the hall of the house.

Paved with cracked marble, the big hall was unfurnished. The windows had been shuttered and the only light came from a bare globe in the ceiling. There was no chair, no table, no sofa, no pictures. The one sign of human occupation was a mop which leant against one wall, but it might have been left there a generation ago by someone hired to tidy up after the furniture-removers had departed."

135

DIARY

Lunch at The Lancaster, Buenos Aires

"But as for joining my aunt in Buenos Aires, my forecast had been too optimistic. There was no one to meet me at the airport, and when I arrived at the Lancaster Hotel I found only my room reserved and a letter. 'I am sorry not to be here to greet you,' she wrote, 'but I have had to move on urgently to Paraguay where an old friend of mine is in some distress. I have left you a ticket for the river-boat. For reasons too complicated to explain now I do not wish you to take a plane to Asunción. I cannot give you an address, but I will see that you are met.'"

Friday, May 3

Buenos Aires. I arrive at dawn on a much-delayed night flight from Miami. Unfortunately, my time in the Argentinian capital has been drastically cut short. After two-hour *siesta* at Hotel Libertador set out to find the celebrated Hotel Lancaster, one of the many locations of *Travels With My Aunt*. But it turns out to be not as interesting as expected. I overcome this by placing it at the front of an entire block of the Avenida Cordoba – a lively strip of Belle Epoque thirties apartments mixing with the neo-Georgian Lancaster. The hotel's interior, on the other hand, is a delightful oasis after recent travels. After spotting a likely pair of Greenesian characters in the elegantly furnished restaurant, decide to take lunch. We're the only occupants. Meal is first-rate: huge shrimps with a fresh green salad, crunchy rolls, followed by a superb compote of huge prunes and peaches. Accompanied by a splendid Argentine Bianchi Chablis and, finally, excellent black coffee. Leave generous tip for waiter: he allowed me to draw my fellow-diners in a sketchbook on my lap, against his implied disapproval.

Sunday, May 5

Asunción, Paraguay. My cab-driver thinks I'm misguided to look for 'old' houses in the Villa Mora neighbourhood of this interesting old capital of land-locked country. 'Why not a new one, señor?' he quips. Unable to make him realize that I really do wish to draw an old house, I pay him off and walk. Although the Villa Mora is a museum of domestic architecture of every period from the later nineteenth century onwards, it is some time before I find an example of a possible millionaire's mansion with padlocked iron gates and 'worn pineapples' over the entrance gateway. Eventually, I succeed and find an opulent example on Avenue Mariscal Lopez, the 'Embassy Row' of Asunción. Here, in a house on the same street, the deposed ex-President of Nicaragua, Somoza, spent his last days of exile prior to his assassination. The house I depict is still in its grandeur, unlike the decrepit one in the novel.

Hotel Lancaster (right), Avenida Cordoba, Buenos Aires

"It was from my aunt, written on stiff aristocratic note-paper bearing simply a scarlet rose and the name Lancaster with no address, like the title of a noble family. Only when I read a little way into the letter did I realize that Lancaster was the name of an hotel. My aunt made no appeal; she simply issued a command, and there was no explanation of her long silence.

'I have decided,' she wrote, 'not to return to Europe and I am giving up my apartment over the Crown and Anchor at the end of the next quarter. I would be glad if you would pack what clothes there may be there and dispose of all the furniture. On second thoughts however keep the photograph of Freetown harbour for me as a memento of dear Wordsworth and bring it with you."

[THE HONORARY CONSUL]

Charlie Fortnum, the 'honorary consul' of a northern province of Argentina, is mistaken for a visiting American Ambassador and kidnapped by a group of Paraguayan revolutionaries who are demanding the release of political prisoners. The mistake is discovered by Dr Plarr when he is called in by Rivas, the leader of the kidnappers, to treat Fortnum. Rivas is a disillusioned priest who was a boyhood friend of Plarr's until Plarr left Paraguay for Argentina with his Paraguayan mother, leaving his English father fighting the forces of oppression. Plarr fails to persuade the kidnappers to release Fortnum and his loyalties are severely tested, for while Rivas is carrying on his father's fight, Charlie is an innocent victim – an ageing, kindly, alcoholic expatriate married to a young ex-prostitute with whom Plarr is having an affair.

The police become suspicious and Plarr is forced to hole up with Fortnum and his captors. It soon becomes plain that the mission is hopeless and it is only a matter of time before they are discovered. While they wait Rivas examines his loss of orthodox Catholic belief and Plarr realizes that his failure to love is a comparable loss. The group are surrounded, Plarr and Rivas shot and Fortnum is rescued.

Fortnum's bumbling and trusting love for his wife has been shaken by his discovery, while in captivity, of her infidelity, but when he finds her grieving for her lover he is grateful that she is capable of love. His experiences have made him aware of the diversity of love and even the motives of the kidnappers had been '. . . love of a kind. People do get caught up by love . . . sooner or later'.

Graham Greene writes:
'I too was warned in Buenos Aires that I would find nothing ever happened in Corrientes. My first morning there I read in bed of a kidnapping of a Consul which threatened to rob me of my idea for a novel: next day a bomb was discovered in the cathedral: the day after that a very popular priest was suspended by the bishop and there were violent protests – a period of peace then followed, but as I left the city by taxi for the airport a crowd had gathered by the riverside. Apparently a whole family had deliberately driven into the Paraná with all the windows closed. So much for nothing happens in Corrientes.'

Puerto de la Balsa, Corrientes, Argentina

Graham Greene writes:
'I needed Fortnum, the "Honorary Consul", to meet Clara his future wife in a Corrientes brothel, but I was told in Buenos Aires that the nearest brothel was some hundred kilometres away. Brothels were now illegal and only private ones existed for the rich. Luckily on arrival in Corrientes I met a knowledgeable Englishman, a representative of Ford cars, who told me, "Nonsense, this is a garrison town" and led me to El Tiburon (The Shark) where the hostess dozed in a deck-chair in the street outside.'

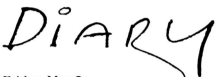

DIARY

Friday, May 3

Buenos Aires, Argentina, 03.00. As Britain is still officially at war with Argentina, I expect questions on entry. But no, I am waved on through by a bewhiskered passport official after he reads my letter of introduction from Señor Fleming, Chargé d'Affaires, Argentina Section at the Brazilian Embassy, London. The letter states the purpose of my visit, citing the magic name of Señor Don Graham Greene.

It is late autumn here. Dawn breaks as the bus speeds towards the distant city along an elevated expressway. Then a dramatic skyline begins to appear: of massed apartment blocks and vast warehouses, culminating in the Art Nouveau turrets of the Club de Pescadores. The sun rises as we enter the inner city and Buenos Aires becomes even more exciting with Parisian-style boulevards and huge histrionic statuary reminiscent of Gustave Doré's monumental vase. It is 08.00 by the time I arrive, exhausted, at the Hotel Libertador.

After a two-hour nap I draw the celebrated Hotel Lancaster for *Travels With My Aunt* (p.137) where I take lunch before returning to the Libertador to check out in good spirits at 15.45. The good spirits are quickly dashed after a mad cab-driver takes me at sixty-five miles per hour to the Aero Parc Aeropuerto. In vain I tell him there's plenty of time. But he only drives faster. South American cab-drivers are fiercely competitive, they

have to be. But this ride is like a car-chase from 'Silents Please' accompanied by a non-stop torrent of verbal abuse at everyone or everything that doesn't or cannot move quickly enough out of his way. Not only does he ask for more than he should be paid, but almost succeeds in spilling the drawings and paper out of my portfolio (which after losing my bag I now carry) by picking it up by the tapes.

My next stop is Corrientes, the setting of *The Honorary Consul*: a port city and busy textile centre on the Paraná River in northern Argentina. As I board the BAC 500 of Aerolineas Argentina, I pass an unexpected reminder of the Falklands War. On the fuselage is the slogan *Las Malvinas son Argentinas* – The Falklands belong to Argentina. Struggle to place my portfolio in convenient place on the crowded plane. A florid fellow-passenger helps, and introduces himself as Jorge Sefarian.

'But call me George,' he booms in impeccable Sloane.

'Obviously,' he continues. 'You're an artist and British but *what* on earth are you doing here in Argentina?'

Delighted to speak my own language again, I reply: 'Following in Graham Greene's footsteps.'

'How *very* interesting,' George rejoins with a deep chuckle. 'Allow me to tell you why. I have an uncle, who has lived in Corrientes for some years, who is a great admirer of Graham Greene. Moreover, he knows all there is to know about his stay in Corrientes when he was collecting material for *The Honorary Consul!* His name is Eduardo Sefarian. Let me give you his telephone number.'

The warmth and import of this unexpected personal encounter stuns me into momentary silence, for Corrientes is a place I have very little information about. I am in luck.

'El Tiburon', Corrientes

Admiral Brown statue, Corrientes

"The bust of an admiral with a homely Irish name."

Paul Hogarth writes:
'Admiral Dr William Brown, a native of County Mayo, was in fact the founder of the Argentinian Navy. In one engagement during the Independence Campaigns of 1810-23 he ran out of shot for his cannon. Undaunted, he resorted to hard Dutch cheese to rout the enemy.'

DIARY

Saturday, May 4

Up early. Call Eduardo Sefarian. His housekeeper informs me he is in his office. So decide to get on with the river scene. Broad slaty-blue Paraná forms the boundary with Paraguay. Corrientes is a bustling frontier city. But it didn't occur to me that the place would be full of armed marines and frontier guards. I get started, studiously deleting gunboats and machine-gun emplacements to concentrate on lovers, street vendors and fishermen.

Eduardo Sefarian returns my call. In a fruity Mancunian accent, he says he would be delighted to show me Graham Greene's Corrientes and picks me up at the hotel. I find him a fit and remarkably astute man in his fifties. We begin the tour even though it's now evening. I find and draw 'the bust of an admiral with a homely Irish name'. He is Admiral Dr William Brown, who fought to liberate Argentina from Spanish rule. After a quick look at the Italian Club, we drive on to the old brothel district near the Avenida Tres de Abril. Here, using the light of a street lamp, I take a sketch of one of the more fascinating glimpses into Greene country – the brothel (now closed) called El Tiburon, or the Shark.

Sunday, May 5

Make early morning trip to depict the *barrio* on the fringe of the town. Here, the group of Paraguayan revolutionaries hide the unfortunate Fortnum, thinking he is the American Ambassador.

"The car drew suddenly and roughly up on the margin of a dirt track. 'We get out here,' Aquino said. After Doctor Plarr had left the car he heard it being backed a few yards. He stood still, letting his eyes grow accustomed to the dark, until he was able to see by starlight the kind of place they had brought him to. It was part of the bidonville *which lay between the city and the bend of the river. The track was almost as wide as a city street, and he could just see a shack made out of dried mud and old petrol cans hidden among the avocados. As his sight cleared he began to make out other huts standing concealed among the trees, like men in ambush. Aquino led him on. The doctor's feet sank more than ankle deep in mud. Even a jeep would have to pass slowly here."*

141

[THE HUMAN FACTOR]

When he was working in South Africa for MI6 Castle had fallen in love with Sarah, a coloured girl, and thus broken the race relations act. A Communist friend helped the girl escape to England where she and Castle married, setting up their home in Berkhamsted with Sarah's son – born from an earlier relationship. Castle's contentment is marred by stress and the need to shield Sarah from the knowledge that he, in order to repay the Communist friend, had agreed to become a double agent.

MI6 have begun to suspect the existence of a double agent and Castle decides to retire, but not before he has passed on information about a secret and irresponsible treaty that is being drawn up between the US, West Germany, Britain and South Africa. This treaty will protect South Africa from the threat of 'invasion' by allowing them to use nuclear tactical weapons which would also have the effect of considerably reducing the black population. Castle gets this information to the Russians but MI6 are now on his trail and he is smuggled to Moscow where he waits apprehensively for the arrival of his family. But Sarah is detained; her son has no passport and she is told by MI6 that any attempt to get him one will alert MI5 who will arrest her for complicity. As a child Castle had always made little profit from swapping his treasures. Now, too, the price he has paid may be too high for anything he has received.

"Castle was usually able to catch the six thirty-five train from Euston. This brought him to Berkhamsted punctually at seven twelve. His bicycle waited for him at the station – he had known the ticket collector for many years and he always left it in his care. Then he rode the longer way home, for the sake of exercise – across the canal bridge, past the Tudor school, into the High Street, past the grey flint parish church which contained the helmet of a crusader, then up the slope of the Chilterns towards his small semi-detached house in King's Road. He always arrived there, if he had not telephoned a warning from London, by half-past seven. There was just time to say good night to the boy and have a whisky or two before dinner at eight.

In a bizarre profession anything which belongs to an everyday routine gains great value – perhaps that was one reason why, when he came back from South Africa, he chose to return to his birthplace: to the canal under the weeping willows, to the school and the ruins of a once-famous castle which had withstood a siege by Prince Louis of France and of which, so the story went, Chaucer had been a Clerk of Works and – who knows? – perhaps an ancestral Castle one of the artisans. It consisted now of only a few grass mounds and some yards of flint wall, facing the canal and the railway line. Beyond was a long road leading away from the town bordered with hawthorn hedges and Spanish chestnut trees until one reached at last the freedom of the Common. Years ago the inhabitants of the town fought for their right to graze cattle upon the Common, but in the twentieth century it was doubtful whether any animal but a rabbit or a goat could have found provender among the ferns, the gorse and the bracken."

Paul Hogarth writes:
'Greene told me that he based his description of Maurice Castle's house on one owned by his aunt: demolished some years ago. Inadvertently, however, I had drawn one of exactly the same type.'

Graham Greene writes:
'I had chosen the name Castle for my principal character because of the presence in his home-town of Berkhamsted Castle. I sent a copy of my book to the former "C", Sir Maurice Oldfield, who was retired and he replied with the amusing comment: "Castle does mean something in that he was one of the cleverest fellows I introduced (we didn't keep him); 'dull' – yes; 'brilliant with files' – who knows – at least not formidable."'

King's Road semis, Berkhamsted

DIARY

Old Compton Street peep shows, Soho

"Castle had taken an earlier train than usual, and he was not due at the office for another three-quarters of an hour. Soho at this hour had still some of the glamour and innocence he remembered from his youth. It was at this corner he had listened for the first time to a foreign tongue, at the small cheap restaurant next door he had drunk his first glass of wine; crossing Old Compton Street in those days had been the nearest he had ever come to crossing the Channel. At nine in the morning the strip-tease clubs were all closed and only the delicatessens of his memory were open. The names against the flat-bells – Lulu, Mimi and the like – were all that indicated the afternoon and evening activities of Old Compton Street. The drains ran with fresh water, and the early housewives passed him under the pale hazy sky, carrying bulging sacks of salami and liverwurst with an air of happy triumph. There was not a policeman in sight, though after dark they would be seen walking in pairs. Castle crossed the peaceful street and entered a bookshop he had frequented for several years now."

Sunday, July 7

Spend baffling but not altogether unrewarding day in Berkhamsted, possibly the prime setting for *The Human Factor*. Many locations in the novel are part of Greene's own past. Berkhamsted is where he grew up.

In Antibes, Greene had suggested I look at *the* castle, close to the railway station. All I can see, however, is a building so completely in ruins, it is impossible to make an effective image. I walk on to the elevated station platform which commands a view of the town. But the castle looks even more of a mess. I clutch my copy of *The Human Factor*, feeling somewhat at a loss but hoping that a solution will emerge.

Maurice Castle, Greene's double-agent hero, has a home in a semi-detached house in King's Road. The idea of depicting such a house, deep in the Home Counties, attracts me so completely that I forgot to ask Greene for the number.

On hearing the sound of a lawnmower, I put my head over a privet hedge. The gardening King's Roader knows the novel well but can't help me. Suggests I telephone a local amateur historian, who has a men's clothing shop in the nearby High Street. He is walking his dog on Berkhamsted Common, says his daughter, and won't be back until 14.00.

For well over an hour, I sample the local beer and sandwiches at three pubs in the High Street: the Crown, the King's Arms and the Swan. All of which claim to be *the* pub where Maurice Castle made his telephone calls. And talking about telephone calls, it's time to telephone the historian again. Eventually, I talk to him. Somewhat impatiently – as he is obviously looking forward to his Sunday lunch – he informs me that such a house doesn't exist. It is nothing, he adds, but a figment of Greene's imagination. Retrace my now weary steps to King's Road, determined to find a suitable house or make it a figment of my imagination. Put myself in Castle's shoes and choose one of two pairs of suburban semis *circa* 1935.

Overton's Restaurant, St James's

"Colonel Daintry had a two-roomed flat in St James's Street which he had found through the agency of another member of the firm. During the war it had been used by MI6 as a rendezvous for interviewing possible recruits. There were only three apartments in the building, which was looked after by an old housekeeper, who lived in a room somewhere out of sight under the roof. Daintry was on the first floor above a restaurant (the noise of hilarity kept him awake until the small hours when the last taxi ground away). Over his head were a retired businessman who had once been connected with the rival wartime service SOE, and a retired general who had fought in the Western Desert. The general was too old now to be seen often on the stairs, but the businessman, who suffered from gout, used to get as far as the Carlton Club across the road. Daintry was no cook and he usually economized for one meal by buying cold chipolatas at Fortnum's. He had never liked clubs; if he felt hungry, a rare event, there was Overton's just below. His bedroom and his bathroom looked out on a tiny ancient court containing a sundial and a silversmith. Few people who walked down St James's Street knew of the court's existence. It was a very discreet flat and not unsuitable for a lonely man."

Graham Greene writes:
'**Daintry occupied my flat on the first floor above a restaurant now Overton's. Field-Marshal Lord Auchinleck had the flat above – not a member of SOE. There was no kitchen, Daintry dealt with that situation much as I did.**'

White's Club, Pall Mall, London

DIARY

Sunday, July 21

Sunday afternoon in London's West End. St James's is where Greene himself had lived in 1947-48 — above Overton's Restaurant – after working for MI6 in the later years of World War II. In the novel it is occupied by Colonel Daintry. Walk on to view White's. Greene himself was a member, as is his character, Daintry. Draw the club as a symbol of privilege and power: an obverse image to that of Castle's semi-detached house in Berkhamsted.

Tuesday, August 6

Old Compton Street, Soho. Draw strip-joints, porno bookshops and young prostitutes. Not as easy it may appear. Sit briefly by an indented window of a male boutique. Owner comes out to ask if he can help me. He returns half an hour later, and tells me if I don't move away, he'll telephone the police. Spectacle of commercial vice is so depressing that I can't remain any longer.

"It took quite a time for Daintry to detach himself from the bar at White's. Buffy even conducted him as far as the steps. A taxi passed. 'You see what I mean,' Buffy said. 'Buses in St James's. No one was safe.' Daintry had no idea what he meant. As he walked down the street towards the palace he was aware that he had drunk more than he had drunk for years at this hour of the day. They were nice fellows, but one had to be careful. He had spoken far too much. About his father, his mother. He walked past Lock's hat shop; past Overton's Restaurant; he halted on the pavement at the corner of Pall Mall. He had overshot the mark – he realized that in time. He turned on his heel and retraced his steps to the door of the flat where his lunch awaited him."

Graham Greene writes:
'I used to lunch often at White's with Evelyn Waugh, a member. Finally I was elected a member and immediately ceased to go there. I am hopelessly unclubable and had already resigned from the Athenaeum and the Reform. The trouble is that after a good bar or a good lunch one finds oneself weakly consenting to be put up for election, trusting in a black ball.'

[DR FISCHER *of* GENEVA]

Jones loves and marries Anna-Luise, the daughter of cruel and eccentric millionaire Fischer of Geneva. Anna-Luise is alienated from her father who has never forgiven her mother for preferring a clerk and their mutual love of music to himself. When Fischer, believing the couple to be lovers, forbade his wife to see her friend again, she lost the will to live and died soon afterwards.

Jones introduces himself to Fischer who invites him to one of his dinner parties, which he uses as vehicles to humiliate a group of rich, greedy, toadying guests who will degrade themselves for more riches. But Jones refuses to play Fischer's game and Fischer recognizes him as someone who will elude him just as his wife and daughter have done. Anna-Luise is killed in a skiing accident and Jones, grief stricken and suicidal, is invited to Fischer's last party. This time the guests will play a form of Russian roulette. Fischer tells them that there are six parcels in a bran tub, five of which contain generous cheques and the other a bomb. Jones wants to play this game and to blow himself up but the bomb eludes him; Fischer has had the last laugh – there is no bomb at all – and at last Jones is humiliated too. Fischer has now had enough of his entertainment and, preferring death to his empty life, he shoots himself.

"The great white house stood above the lake like a Pharaoh's tomb. It dwarfed my car, and the bell seemed to tinkle absurdly in the depths of the enormous grave. Albert opened the door. For some reason he was dressed in black. Had Doctor Fischer put his servant into mourning in his place? The black suit seemed to have changed his character for the better. He made no show of not recognizing me. He didn't sneer at me, but led the way promptly up the great marble staircase."

"I took a day off from work and drove down by the lake, but I very nearly turned back when I saw the extent of the grounds, the silver birches and the weeping willows and the great green cascade of the lawn in front of a pillared portico. A greyhound lay asleep like an heraldic emblem. I felt I should have gone to the tradesmen's entrance."

The Villa Prangins

Graham Greene writes:
'This house was found on the shores of the lake by the producer of the film Dr Fischer. *It seems to me perfect for the home of the doctor.'*

DIARY

Wednesday, October 2

I'm on an early morning flight to Geneva. I haven't visited Switzerland for some years, and of course the country remains neat, tidy and laid back. The epitome of a bourgeois republic insulated from the sorrows and violence of our time. Here, there's always space to park a car and no one takes the slightest interest in what you may be up to.

Stay at a charming lakeside hotel, the Clos du Sadex on the outskirts of Nyon. Telephone Monsieur Claude Soupert, new owner of Villa Prangins, which Greene suggests should be the 'great white house' of Dr Fischer. The Villa was used by BBC television for their film version of *Dr Fischer of Geneva*. Originally, it belonged to Prince Gérôme Napoléon and, later, Emperor Charles I of Austria. There's been a change of ownership since I was given permission. So I have to wait for confirmation that the new owner will also agree.

Follow complicated instructions to locate the Villa. Dusk slowly gathers as I speed through a silent forest. After two kilometres turn into enormous drive. A large mansion built in the French Empire style faces Lake Léman (Lake Geneva). The place seems unoccupied and I get to work. Owls flit about to deepen the already eerie atmosphere. I'm startled at the appearance of the white face of a caretaker at one of the many tall ground-floor windows. Drive back through the now darkling forest thinking how appropriate a setting it was for the Doctor's dinner party gamesmanship.

Hotel des Trois Couronnes, Vevey

148

Nestlé factory, Vevey

"Anna-Luise and her millionaire father inhabited a great white mansion in the classical style by the lakeside at Versoix outside Geneva while I worked as a translator and letter-writer in the immense chocolate factory of glass in Vevey."

149

DiARY

Thursday, October 3

Breakfast on terrace. Lake magical in the early morning mist with sun breaking through. Swans and coots swim about, gulls and cormorants skim the water hunting for fish. Reluctantly leave for Vevey, to depict the giant Nestlé headquarters overlooking Lake Léman on the Avenue de Savoie. This is the original of the 'immense chocolate factory of glass' where Jones, the hero of Greene's 'black entertainment' and lover of Dr Fischer's daughter, Anna-Luise, is employed as a translator. As I work, I recall a previous visit to Vevey in 1967: an assignment for *Fortune* to portray the high command of this world-wide food-producing organization. Its two remarkable managing directors at the time, Jean Corthésy and Enrico Bignami, divided their responsibilities. One running day-to-day operations, the other concentrating on long-range planning: an interdependence which prompted the idea of drawing them as Siamese-like twins. Recalling, too, the hygienic interior of the vast plant, I can only appreciate more fully Greene's brilliant descriptive inferences.

La Nouvelle Chevaline, Vevey

"So it was that things began for us, but a
month of stray meetings in Vevey and of
watching classic films in a small cinema in
Lausanne half way between our homes
was needed before I realized we were both in
love . . ."

DIARY

Friday, October 4

I'm staying at the Hotel des Trois Couronnes, a vast Victorian Grand Hotel with corridors almost twenty metres wide. It's my birthday and I need to feel good. Besides, the place is full of the sort of characters or 'toadies' who attended Dr Fischer's famous dinner-parties, and whom he loved to torment.

Drive out to nearby ski-resort of Les Paccots, the setting of the tragic climax of the novella. Here, seated by the window of the Hotel Corbetta, Jones learns of the fatal accident which befalls Anna-Luise while skiing. Facing the hotel is a huge ominous pine forest above which a ski-lift vanishes towards a steep mountain slope to infinity.

"I suppose there is a day in most lives when every trivial detail is held in the memory as though stamped in wax. Such a day proved for me to be the last day of the year – a Saturday. The night before we had decided to drive up in the morning to Les Paccots if the weather proved fine enough for Anna-Luise to ski. There had been a slight thaw on Friday, but Friday night it was freezing. We would go early before the slopes were crowded and have lunch together at the hotel there."

Les Paccots

[MONSIGNOR QUIXOTE]

Padre Quixote is elevated from his humble position of parish priest to that of Monsignor as the result of a visit from a Roman bishop who is impressed by the quality of his hospitality. His own envious bishop recommends that his elevation is more suitable to a bigger parish or even a mission, and that he should leave his beloved El Toboso.

Quixote's friend, a Communist ex-mayor, Zancas, known affectionately by Quixote as Sancho, loses the local election and is redundant too. The two friends decide to take a short holiday together, travelling in Quixote's trusty Seat 600, *Rocinante*.

Theirs is a voyage of discovery; what might have seemed an immense philosophical and religious gap between the two men is bridged by their mutual respect, and the ideas of Marx, Descartes and Jone are well absorbed together with the local wine.

Quixote's behaviour comes to the attention of the Catholic authorities, and some of his actions which have seemed to him sensible and Christian do in fact question basic tenets of the Catholic church and are construed as deviant and demented. Quixote is eventually kidnapped by the local clergy; he has tilted at too many windmills which in *his* age are represented by the Spanish Guardia. The unholy alliance of the Guardia and the church allow Quixote to be mortally wounded, and in a delirious act of true – and Quixotic – communion, he dies.

"It needed a great deal of courage for Father Quixote to write to the bishop and an even greater courage to open the letter which in due course he received in reply. The letter began abruptly 'Monsignor' – and the sound of the title was like acid on the tongue. 'El Toboso,' the bishop wrote, 'is one of the smallest parishes in my diocese, and I cannot believe that the burden of your duties has been a very heavy one. However, I am ready to grant your request for a period of repose and I am despatching a young priest, Father Herrera, to look after El Toboso in your absence. I trust that at least you will delay your holiday until you are fully satisfied that Father Herrera is aware of all the problems which may exist in your parish, so that you can leave your people with complete confidence in his care. The defeat of the Mayor of El Toboso in the recent election seems to indicate that the tide is turning at last in the proper direction and perhaps a young priest with the shrewdness and discretion of Father Herrera (he won golden opinions as well as a doctorate in Moral Theology at Salamanca) will be better able to take advantage of the current than an older man. As you will guess I have written to the Archbishop with regard to your future, and I have small doubt that by the time you return from your holiday we will have found you a sphere of action more suitable than El Toboso and carrying a lesser burden of duties for a priest of your age and rank.'"

Calle Quixote, El Toboso

Graham Greene writes:
'*For some six years before this book was published I had been travelling the roads of Spain between Madrid and El Toboso and the Monastery of Osera in Galicia with my friend Father Leopoldo Durán and the chosen driver from among his friends. The idea of the book was actually born in Portugal over two and a half bottles of Vinho Verde which brought to mind a problem of belief – in the Trinity.'*

155

DIARY

Tuesday, September 17

Lunch at Madrid's Barajas Airport with Father Leopoldo Duran (Greene's friend and companion on frequent travels in Spain). Father Duran in good form. Bubbles with helpful suggestions. Arranges for stay with Trappist monks at Osera, Galicia.

In *Monsignor Quixote*, the good Monsignor drives a little Seat 600 named after his famous name-sake's horse, Rocinante. He is accompanied by his friend and sparring partner, the ex-Communist mayor of El Toboso who goes by the name of Sancho Panza. I am accompanied by my son, Toby, who drives a rented Renault TSE as we have to follow their itinerary in little more than five days.

Soon we are on our way to the first location, the village of El Toboso in La Mancha. Set amidst vast parched fields and huge square vineyards, the village has largely kept its ancient character. It was here that Cervantes had his Don Quixote discover the incomparable 'Dulcinea', daughter of a local peasant, whom he elects to be the mistress of his heart, endowed with every virtue.

Towards sunset, El Toboso becomes animated. Peasants appear in baggy black trousers and straw hats. Dignified old folks sit on battered chairs. Young wives bustle about on errands or to shop. Some of this street life goes into the one drawing I have time to make before we move on to Alcazar de San Juan: a bustling market town nearby. Here we stay the night in a simple hotel following the illustrious example (for once) of the Monsignor and Sancho.

"More than an hour passed in silence. Then the
Mayor spoke again. 'What is upsetting you,
friend?'
  'We have just left La Mancha and nothing
seems safe any more.'
  'Not even your faith?'
  It was a question which Father Quixote did
not bother to answer."

Windmills near Alcazar de San Juan

157

DiARY

Wednesday, September 18

Alcazar de San Juan surrounded by vast austere landscape. Here and there clusters of ruined windmills line ridges of dusty khaki hills like rotten teeth. I get a drawing of one such cluster, supposedly Dulcinea's mills, called Sendero de los Molinos, before we continue on our drive north. We pass through one Manchegan village after another. Even the poorest has a Bar Cervantes and, usually, a bust of the writer. The more affluent boast the occasional equestrian statue of the Knight with the faithful Sancho at his side.

By midday, we are well on our way to the Sierra de Guadarrama: a wild and craggy region of oak and pine forests and rushing mountain streams. We pass through Guadarrama, the most easterly of the northern gates to Madrid and scene of heavy fighting during the Civil War. Our next stop is the Valle de los Caidos, the Valley of the Fallen. Shortly before lunch we drive through an elaborate gateway as though entering some strange kingdom damned to exist apart from all others. The valley is the site of a grandiose mausoleum built by Republican prisoners of Franco's forces for the Nationalist dead of the Civil War. Franco himself is buried here in a huge basilica, as are 40,000 soldiers. Most of the visitors are now over thirty-five: widows, relatives of the fallen and tourists brought by fleets of tour-buses. An immense cross towers above, flanked by gigantic statues of the Evangelists and the four cardinal virtues.

We enter Segovia as the sun sets through the arches of the Roman aqueduct: a most dramatic spectacle. This most picturesque of the cities of Old Castile is perched on an enormous rock, crowded with ancient houses and gold-hued Romanesque churches. Segovia is the city of Daniel Zuloaga (1852-1921), Spain's most famous painter before Picasso. We end a marathon day of driving and drawing at a restaurant *tipico Castellana*, that of Señor Jose Maria, off the Plaza de Franco serving good regional food.

Tomb of Miguel de Unamuno, Campo Santo, Salamanca

"*They returned to Rocinante.*
'*Where do we go from here, Sancho?*'
'*We go to the cemetery. You will find his tomb rather different from the Generalissimo's.*'
It was a rough road out to the cemetery on the extreme edge of the city – not a smooth road for a hearse to travel. The body, Father Quixote thought as Rocinante groaned when the gears changed, would have had a good shaking up before it reached the quiet ground, but as he soon discovered there had been no quiet ground left for a new body – the earth was fully occupied by the proud tombs of generations before. At the gates they were given a number, as in the cloakroom of a museum or a restaurant, and they walked down the long white wall in which boxes had been inserted half a dozen deep until they reached number 340.
'*I prefer this to the Generalissimo's mountain,' Sancho said. 'When I am alone, I sleep more easily in a small bed.*'"

Santa Cruz del Valle de Los Caidos

"'That's more or less the same thing, isn't it. Where are we, Sancho?'

'This is the Valley of the Fallen, father. Here your friend Franco like a pharaoh planned to be buried. More than a thousand prisoners were forced to excavate his tomb.'

'Oh yes, I remember, and they were given their liberty in return.'

'For hundreds it was the liberty of death. Shall you say a prayer here, father?'

'Of course. Why not? Even if it was the tomb of Judas – or Stalin – I'd say a prayer.'

They parked the car at a cost of sixty pesetas and came to the entrance. What a rock it would need, Father Quixote thought, to close this enormous tomb. At the entrance a metal grille was decorated with the statues of forty Spanish saints, and inside stretched a hall the size of a cathedral nave, the walls covered with what appeared to be sixteenth-century tapestries. 'The Generalissimo insisted on the whole brigade of saints,' the Mayor said. The visitors and their voices were diminished by the size of the hall, and it seemed a long walk to the altar at the end under a great dome.

'A remarkable engineering feat,' the Mayor said, 'like the pyramids. And it needed slave labour to accomplish it.'

'As in your Siberian camps.'

'Russian prisoners labour at least for the future of their country. This was for the glory of one man.'

They walked at a slow pace towards the altar, passing chapel after chapel. No one in this richly decorated hall felt the need to lower his voice, and yet the voices sounded as soft as whispers in the immensity. It was difficult to believe that they were walking inside a mountain."

The wicked priest's house, Beariz, Galicia

Paul Hogarth writes:
'According to Father Durán, Greene based his wicked priest – whom Monsignor Quixote accuses of blasphemy – on one that once lived in this house in Beariz.'

DiARY

Thursday, September 19

Leave Segovia for Salamanca. It is more worldly than Segovia, more metropolitan. During the Civil War the city was Franco's base – the home of the Head of State, the Falangist organizations, the Foreign Office, the embassies and political staffs of Germany and Italy. Depict wall interment of the writer Miguel de Unamuno in the Santo Campo. Like Monsignor Quixote and Sancho, we reflect on the contrast between the ostentatious tomb of Franco and this simple resting-place of one of Europe's great literary figures.

Friday, September 20

Long drive to Osera in Galicia, entering a sub-alpine landscape of picturesque poor village. Stone walls divide the fields like in Cumbria. Arrive at the Monasterio de Osera, the scene of the final episode of the novel. We are given a warm welcome by the monks, and escorted to Cell suite 19. We are informed that Greene occupied Cell 14. The monastery is a huge complex of buildings ranging from the Romanesque to the Baroque in style. The monks are Trappists, a reformed Cistercian Order, established in 1664 at La Trappe, Normandy. They observe an extremely austere regime involving silence except for confession and choral song. Greene says they're the Stalinists of the Catholic faith.

Decide to make reconnaissance with the object of making a big drawing before sunset. We must be back, guestmaster warns, when the bell tolls. The pervasively Medieval ambience brings to mind the scenes of monastic life painted by William Frederick Yeames, especially his *Administration of Discipline in the Chapter of a Monastery* or, as the Victorian artist originally called his picture, *Exorcising by Bell, Book and Candle.*

Unfortunately for me, the local mosquito population appear in strength and mount an offensive; defying all attempts to keep them at bay with insect repellent spray-cans. Gathering dusk only increases their number as I strive to complete the drawing. Suddenly, the bell tolls! Covered with bites, I nonetheless continue working as I must have this strange twilight in my drawing.

We return to find ourselves locked out. Passing monk working on monastery's farm says we must wait until vespers are over to gain re-admittance. Chastened by the experience, we return to our cell-suite along candle-lit corridors. White-robed monks stand immobile at mullioned windows immersed in deep reflection. The day ends with a lively dinner. The guests include Padre Santos, a parish priest, and Alexandro Vacquez, a middle-aged painter. Both are seeking rest and 'spiritual renewal'. We expect a prayer before eating. None are forthcoming, however. Laymen, priests and monks tuck into the feast before them with Rabelaisian gusto.

Fiesta time, Salamanca

The Roman Aqueduct, Segovia

"*The great Roman aqueduct of Segovia loomed ahead of them, casting a long shadow in the evening light.*

They found a lodging in a small albergue not far from the Church of St Martin – that name again – the name by which he always thought of her. She seemed closer to him then than in her trappings as a saint or under her sentimental nickname of the Little Flower. He would even sometimes address her in his prayers as Señorita Martin as though the family name might catch her ear through all the thousands of incantations addressed to her in all tongues by the light of candles before the plaster image."

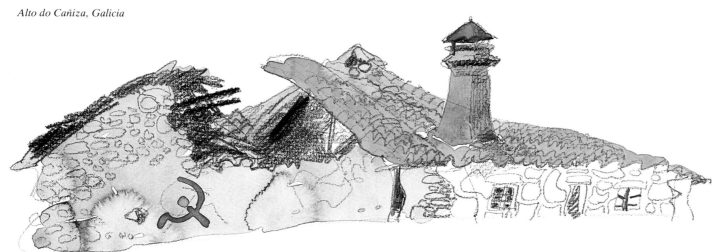

Alto do Cañiza, Galicia

"The great grey edifice of the Osera monastery stretches out almost alone within a trough of the Galician hills. A small shop and a bar at the very entrance of the monastery grounds make up the whole village of Osera. The carved exterior which dates from the sixteenth century hides the twelfth-century interior – an imposing stairway, perhaps twenty metres wide, up which a platoon could march shoulder to shoulder, leads to long passages lined with guest rooms above the central courtyard and the cloisters. Almost the only sound during the day is the ring of hammers where half a dozen workmen are struggling to repair the ravages of seven centuries. Sometimes a white-robed figure passes rapidly by on what is apparently a serious errand, and in the dark corners loom the wooden figures of popes and of the knights whose order founded the monastery. They take on an appearance of life, as sad memories do, when the dark has fallen. A visitor has the impression of an abandoned island which has been colonized only recently by a small group of adventurers, who are now trying to make a home in the ruins of a past civilization.

The doors of the church, which open on to the little square before the monastery, are closed except during visiting hours and at the time of Sunday Masses, but the monks have their private staircase which leads from the corridor, where the guest rooms lie, down to the great nave as large as many a cathedral's. Only during visiting hours or when guests are present do human voices sound among the ancient stones, as though a pleasure boat has deposited a few tourists on the shore."

"They drive very slowly, looking out for a tree which would give them shade, for the late sun was slanting low across the fields, driving the shadows into patches far too thin for two men to sit in them at ease. Finally, under the ruined wall of an outhouse, which belonged to an abandoned farm, they found what they needed. Someone had painted a hammer and sickle crudely in red upon the crumbling stone."

DIARY

Saturday, September 21

And so on to Beariz, the location of the confrontation with the 'Mexicans' or locals who have returned from Latin America with small fortunes. Monsignor Quixote, it will be recalled, interrupts an annual festival where an effigy of the Blessed Virgin is plastered with banknotes. In a scene in which he emulates Christ driving the money-changers out of the temple, the Monsignor furiously tears the notes from the effigy.

We only see peasant women in big floppy hats driving cows home for milking. We continue to Las Regardas. Search for the casita and vineyard of Señor Antonio Noquerias, the Señor Diego of the novel. We are taken to his house along a maze of steep twisting lanes. We visit his fruitful vineyard before a magnificent impromptu lunch with his relatives. We are generously served with white wine and ham, followed by fried eggs, then coffee and brandy. After the meal, toasts are made to life, love and happiness, and 'Señor Grayhem Grinne.'

Monasterio de Santa María de Osera

[THE TENTH MAN]

A group of French hostages are faced by the Nazis with reprisal. One man in ten is to be shot. The hostages draw lots and the loser, Chavel, a middle-aged lawyer, panics and offers his country house and possessions to anyone who will take his place. Janvier sacrifices himself for he is sickly and wants to secure the future of his mother and sister.

At the end of the war Chavel, finding himself unemployable and homeless, visits his beloved house at St Jean de Brinac under an assumed name posing as Janvier's friend, and is taken on by Janvier's sister as a gardener. The sister is bitter about her brother's death. She does not appreciate her wealth and blames Chavel-the-coward for the death of her brother.

Carosse, a collaborator on the run, takes refuge at the house — posing, to Chavel's surprise, as Chavel. The sister's anger is defused by the sudden death of her mother and while she is bewildered by grief she allows Carosse – a consummate actor — to ingratiate himself. Carosse then takes advantage of information about a new decree which makes changes of property during the occupation illegal, meaning the house has reverted to Chavel, and Carosse thus claims it together with its dispossessed mistress. Chavel threatens to expose Carosse to the local resistance leader – his childhood friend – who would also identify the real Chavel. Carosse shoots Chavel and disappears. Chavel, dying, feels he has 'taken a lot of trouble to delay a recurring occasion'.

"Strange ideas grow in prison and the mayor and the engine driver drew together yet more intimately: it was as though they feared that the Germans chose deliberately the men with watches to rob them of time: the mayor even began to suggest to his fellow prisoners that the two remaining timepieces should be kept hidden rather than that all should lose their services, but when he began to put this idea into words the notion suddenly seemed to resemble cowardice and he broke off in mid-sentence."

Maison de la Santé, Paris

DIARY

Monday, October 14

Besides being a location for *Travels With My Aunt*, Paris is a setting for much of *The Tenth Man*. Travelling from Boulogne I search for a possible candidate for Jean-Louis Charlot's country house at St Jean de Brinac. This takes me through Lisle d'Adam and St Germain-en-Laye. But the style of Charlot's house is so Breton and not Ile-de-France that I abandon the quest for the time being. I'm staying with an historian friend in Paris. Perhaps she might advise me. Subsequently she does and helps me find a house in Brittany, which I later draw.

Gare de l'Ouest, Paris

The House at St Jean de Brinac

"A man calling himself Jean-Louis Charlot came up the drive of the house at St Jean de Brinac.

Everything was the same as he had remembered it and yet very slightly changed, as if the place and he had grown older at different rates. Four years ago he had shut the house up, and while for him time had almost stood still, here time had raced ahead. For several hundred years the house had grown older almost imperceptibly; years were little more than a changed shadow on the brickwork. Like an elderly woman the house had been kept in flower – the face lifted at the right moment: now in four years all that work had been undone: the lines broke through the enamel which had not been renewed.

In the drive the gravel was obscured by weeds: a tree had fallen right across the way, and though somebody had lopped the branches for firewood, the trunk still lay there to prove that for many seasons no car had driven up to the house. Every step was familiar to the bearded man who came cautiously round every bend like a stranger. He had been born here: as a child he had played games of hide and seek in the bushes: as a boy he had carried the melancholy and sweetness of first love up and down the shaded drive. Ten yards further on there would be a small gate on to the path which led between heavy laurels to the kitchen garden.

The gate had gone: only the posts showed that memory hadn't failed him. Even the nails which had held the hinges had been carefully extracted to be used elsewhere for some more urgent purpose. He turned off the drive: he didn't want to face the house yet: like a criminal who returns to the scene of his crime or a lover who returns to haunt the place of farewell, he moved in intersecting circles: he didn't dare to move in a straight line and finish his pilgrimage prematurely, with nothing more to do for ever after."

DIARY

Tuesday, October 15

Decide to make the Maison de la Santé the prime setting. After all, besides the house at Brinac, it features significantly in the novel. The Santé, or some similar grim gaol, is where the Gestapo would have held Charlot and his fellow-hostages. Despite its great size (covering an entire city block) the Santé isn't easy to find these days. Towering blocks of flats now screen off the view of the Santé which was once a feature of the fourteenth *arrondissement* from the elevated section of the Métro. Then, suddenly it comes into view, as one turns into the Rue de la Santé. A huge umber bulk surrounded by high walls discoloured by patches of black grime.

Immediately feel I *must* draw the place: so perfectly does the Santé symbolize imprisonment and loss of liberty. But this isn't going to be at all easy. Guards patrol each corner with walkie-talkies. Nothing escapes their surveillance as each guard has an uninterrupted view of every street around the vast prison. As I walk around to find a possible vantage point, I spot a *pissoir*, which also features in the novel. What luck, I say to myself. One by one, the traditional features of Paris slowly disappear. Few of the many public urinals remain which once punctuated the streets of the French capital. This one near the Santé is retained because a modern and therefore enclosed convenience would only serve as an illicit rendezvous for criminals anxious to liberate their unfortunate colleagues.

I haven't even got as far as taking out my sketchbook when a burly guard appears to make a brutally frank gesture that I'm to get on my way *tout de suite*. Continue walking, feeling that I've blown my chances. The burly guard whispers into his walkie-talkie, informing the next guard who pretends not to look at me as I re-enter the first street of my promenade. At the corner of the Rue Messieur, I unexpectedly find a good vantage point in a small *impasse* or alley. Another guard is already on his way over. Deciding that diplomacy might just win the day, I tell him I'm a *'peintre anglais'* and show him my Boulogne drawings.

'Je suis Boulonnais,' he replies, not batting an eyelid. Feeling that the battle has been lost, I play my trump card. I tell him about *The Tenth Man*: that the hero Charlot was imprisoned here by *les Allemands*. He nods gravely and to my amazement tells me he has read the novel.

'Ah, Graam Grinne!' he smiles, *'un grand écrivain'*. Nods his approval, and strides away. Such is the power of a writer, and his book, I reflect, that it even overrides the sentimental appeal of a policeman's home town.

"Nevertheless no collaborator felt a more hunted man than Charlot, for his past was equally shameful: he could explain to no one how he had lost his money – if indeed it was not already known. He was haunted at street corners by the gaze from faintly familiar faces and driven out of buses by backs he imagined he knew; deliberately he moved into a Paris that was strange to him. His Paris had always been a small Paris: its arc had been drawn to include his flat, the law courts, the Opéra, the Gare de l'Ouest and one or two restaurants.

"'Well, Jules,' Charlot said.
    The shallow eyes flickered disapproval: the man only liked his intimates – the payers, Charlot thought – to call him by his name.
    'You don't remember me, Jules,' Charlot said."

GAZETTEER

The gazetteer includes those places, cities or countries visited or depicted by Paul Hogarth, or which are mentioned by him and Graham Greene in their respective texts. Actual names of places or streets are followed in brackets by those given by Graham Greene where they differ.

ALSO BY PAUL HOGARTH

GRAHAM GREENE BIBLIOGRAPHY

FICTION

THE MAN WITHIN *(Heinemann)*	1929	Copyright 1929 by Graham Greene
THE NAME OF ACTION *(Heinemann)*	1930	Copyright 1930 by Graham Greene
RUMOUR AT NIGHTFALL *(Heinemann)*	1931	Copyright 1931 by Graham Greene
STAMBOUL TRAIN *(Heinemann)*	1932	© renewed Graham Greene 1960
IT'S A BATTLEFIELD *(Heinemann)*	1934	Copyright 1934 by Graham Greene. © Graham Greene, 1962
THE BEAR FELL FREE *(Grayson)*	1935	Copyright 1935 by Graham Greene
THE BASEMENT ROOM *(Cresset Press)*	1935	Copyright 1935 by Graham Greene

[Reprinted in a different selection as *Nineteen Stories* (Heinemann) 1947 and as *Twenty-One Stories* (Heinemann) 1954]

ENGLAND MADE ME *(Heinemann)*	1935	Copyright 1935 by Graham Greene
A GUN FOR SALE *(Heinemann)*	1936	Copyright 1936 by Graham Greene. © Graham Greene, 1973
BRIGHTON ROCK *(Heinemann)*	1938	Copyright 1938 by Graham Greene. © Graham Greene, 1966, 1970
THE CONFIDENTIAL AGENT *(Heinemann)*	1939	Copyright 1939 by Graham Greene. © Graham Greene, 1971
THE POWER AND THE GLORY *(Heinemann)*	1940	Copyright 1940 by Graham Greene. © Graham Greene, 1968, 1971
THE MINISTRY OF FEAR *(Heinemann)*	1943	© Graham Greene, 1943, 1973
THE HEART OF THE MATTER *(Heinemann)*	1948	Copyright 1948 by Graham Greene. © Graham Greene, 1971
THE THIRD MAN & THE FALLEN IDOL *(Heinemann)*	1950	Copyright by Graham Greene 1935, 1950. © Graham Greene, 1963, 1977
THE END OF THE AFFAIR *(Heinemann)*	1951	© Graham Greene 1951
THE QUIET AMERICAN *(Heinemann)*	1955	© Graham Greene, 1955, 1973
LOSER TAKES ALL *(Heinemann)*	1955	© Graham Greene, 1954, 1955
OUR MAN IN HAVANA *(Heinemann)*	1958	© William Heinemann Ltd, 1958
A BURNT-OUT CASE *(Heinemann)*	1961	© Graham Greene, 1960, 1961
A SENSE OF REALITY *(Bodley Head)*	1963	© Graham Greene, 1963, 1972

[contains four stories]

THE COMEDIANS *(Bodley Head)*	1966	© Graham Greene, 1965-66
MAY WE BORROW YOUR HUSBAND? *(Bodley Head)*	1967	© Graham Greene, 1967
TRAVELS WITH MY AUNT *(Bodley Head)*	1969	© Graham Greene, 1969
COLLECTED STORIES *(Bodley Head)*	1972	© Graham Greene, 1954, 1956, 1963, 1966, 1967, 1972
THE HONORARY CONSUL *(Bodley Head)*	1973	© Graham Greene, 1973
THE HUMAN FACTOR *(Bodley Head)*	1978	© Graham Greene, 1978
DR FISCHER OF GENEVA *(Bodley Head)*	1980	© Graham Greene, 1980
MONSIGNOR QUIXOTE *(Bodley Head)*	1982	© Graham Greene, 1982
THE TENTH MAN *(Bodley Head and Anthony Blond)*	1985	© MGM/UA Home Entertainment Group, 1985 Introduction and revised text © Graham Greene, 1985

TRAVEL & AUTOBIOGRAPHY

JOURNEY WITHOUT MAPS *(Heinemann)*	1936	Copyright by Graham Greene 1936
THE LAWLESS ROADS *(Heinemann)*	1939	Copyright by Graham Greene 1939
IN SEARCH OF A CHARACTER:		
TWO AFRICAN JOURNALS *(Bodley Head)*	1961	© Graham Greene, 1961
A SORT OF LIFE *(Bodley Head)*	1971	© Graham Greene, 1971
WAYS OF ESCAPE *(Bodley Head)*	1980	© Graham Greene, 1980

GRAHAM GREENE COUNTRY

CANADA

U.S.

Atlantic

Mexico

Gulf of Mexico

(1)

(2) (3)

Caribbean Sea

Pacific Ocean

SOUTH AMERICA

(1) THE POWER AND THE GLORY 1940 *Mexico*
(2) OUR MAN IN HAVANA 1958 *Cuba*
(3) THE COMEDIANS 1966 *Haiti*
(4) TRAVELS WITH MY AUNT 1969
Paraguay and Argentina
(5) THE HONORARY CONSUL 1973
Argentina

PARAGUAY

ARGENTINIA

(4)

(5)

Ocean

(4)